CONTENT

This book is mostly fiction, the characters being my relatives who lived in the times depicted. However, actual incidents are also included, based on word-of-mouth stories handed down through the generations, such as family Bibles, journals, postcards, photos, and other memorabilia. The conversations, thoughts, and events portrayed in this work are entirely a product of the author's imagination in an attempt to bring to life my ancestors' experiences for future generations.

Book Design and Layout by Russell Shuler.

ACKNOWLEDGEMENTS

Vina's story is a collaboration of many. The words are mine, but the spirit, motivation and final product is the result of many of my family and friends' constant encouragement. Notably, Kay Eaton, who hounded me for years to write a book and to ask God for help. Jill LaForge Jones, a long-time friend and very respected author who inspired me, gave me the tools to start and stayed with me editing and honing my new skills to make it readable. She made me believe I could do this. Annie Campbell, friend, historian and retired English teacher, who selflessly helped me research, challenged me with questions, improved my grammar and perspectives without grading my papers. My mother, Ruth Louise Summers, who left volumes of her memories of events and stories told that helped me bring Vina to life. I am especially grateful to my husband, Patrick, who cooked, cleaned and did laundry while I followed this passion. Thank you, Lord, and thank you Nana for the inspiration.

(pronounced vīn ä)

FOREWORD

By Author

History can only be understood by understanding the times in which incidents occurred. I inherited over 200 Victorian Post Cards in beautiful ornate albums saved by my maternal grandmother. By the time I received them, over a hundred years later, the albums had deteriorated into dust, but the cards were well preserved. Short, quick notes written in pencil to and from family and friends that she held close, can still be read. Each post card is a work of art and a sentiment of caring: good news, bad news, lighthearted jokes, admonishments and declarations of love. I rescued the cards from the dust and preserved them and tucked them away. I cherish the post cards and in recent years, I have come to think of them as the "texts" of a past generation.

I thought about them occasionally and even knowing much about my mother's family, I had a few questions. While visiting my mother's sister, Rosemary McBride, then in her nineties in a nursing home, and as sharp as ever, I asked her why my grandmother, Nana, had so many last names. "You don't know about the kidnapping?", she answered. I was speechless, never having known of such an event. She added that "things" like that just weren't talked about back then. She relayed the few details she knew, and I jotted them down when I arrived home. That was in 2013, over eleven years ago. I occasionally told the story as cocktail conversation, but it stayed in my mind. I found it difficult to reconcile the Nana that I knew as a child of twelve with a woman who had such a unique history. The women in my family have always been strong, but I never thought about the source of that strength and tenacity, until recently.

My mother was a writer and has left many histories and family stories for future generations to read. In all of her many writings, there is nothing to hint at the kidnapping or the missing 14 years of her mother Vina's life. Having known my grandmother and even as a child feeling her strength, I felt compelled to make sure her story was told. My intention was to write a quick essay to tuck in one of my mother's many volumes. This grew from a Saturday afternoon project to an intense four months. I have loved every minute of research, rediscovered photographs, and getting to know Vina, and I hope readers will also.

PART ONE

Amanda Melvina Nichols Knight, 1859-1892

CHAPTER ONE

Amanda Melvina Nichols Knight

One hundred seventy-nine miles to travel from my home as I had known it. One hundred and seventy-nine miles from those I have loved and those I have buried there. My sweet baby, Benjamin, barely two years old and recently left in the ground that I loved but wouldn't sustain us. His older brother Moody buried nearby. I felt every rut, every rock, every pebble, and every mile while sitting on a wooden plank in our cramped covered wagon. I was surrounded by the damp mildew smell of old stained canvas ,and the creaking sound of wood straining to hold the wagon together with all of the possessions we owned. Crowded with sacks of staples we had brought for food, tools to build a home, a few blankets, my prized iron stove, three sons ten, eight, and five, and a multitude of prayers for a better life. My beloved, headstrong husband and fourteen-year-old son, Risdon, sat up front to steer the horses. I held my Bible in my lap to protect it and receive its strength. I tried to entertain my boys with songs and stories to help the time pass. I told them about my father, their grandfather, who was named Risdon Daniel Nichols. He fought in the infantry in the Civil War, and I concocted stories about his bravery. He was captured and died in a POW camp, but I left that part out. Our possessions shifted constantly in the tight space battering me and taking away what optimism I had.

It was early April 1889, and the weather was still mild as we headed North. It was welcome because we had survived the past winter with failed crops and much sadness. I was still grieving Benjamin, and the bit of sunshine on my face was healing and gave me hope. Our last crops had finally yielded enough to get a little bit ahead. There were lots of families like ours. We were blessed to still have two horses and an old covered wagon. James even made several extra wheels to carry with us. Many were on foot and carrying or dragging their belongings. Some travelers looked more desperate than we were. With every mile, there were more men or families or even a few single women all with the same purpose—to own their own land. No one seemed to care that it was land that had been ceded by the Indians to the government after the Civil War, only that the government was making it available to homesteaders like us.

James was sure that with lots of prayers, healthy sons, hard work, ingenuity, and a lot of luck that we could meet the requirements to homestead. In only five years, we would own one hundred and sixty acres, but I thought to myself that for every gruesome mile of this trip, we would own an acre of land, and still, I wasn't convinced that it was going to be a good trade for me. If the weather held out, we would make almost ten miles a day. We would make camp and settle in for the night. Usually, we were joined by other families who felt as we did, that it was safer for us to be in groups. The Indians were still very unknown to us, and we had heard fearsome stories, but most agreed it was worth the risk.

The women cooked and got acquainted while the children ran around playing and hollering. The men had made campfires and were taking care of animals, sharing stories, and a few had brought whiskey. Fear of the unknown was palatable. This was considered a last chance by many, and nerves led to tempers that erupted unexpectedly. Occasionally a fight broke out among both strangers and friends. The possibility of Indian encounters tended to sober the crowd before the men became too rowdy. Several of the men offered to stand watch over our camp at night. I suppose that gave comfort to many of us. We were told that the Creek and Seminole Indians, whose former land we were headed for, had been paid for that land that now was made available to folks like us. But we also heard that some of the tribes were not happy with that Federal Treaty, and it was possible that they would make trouble for us. Thankfully, we were blessed with only friendly encounters even though the threat of the Indians' possible resistance was intimidating.

The actual date of the so-called Oklahoma Land Rush was April 22, at noon. We had come from the piney woods of Texas where there were lots of trees and farms. But the soil had not been good to us, and we had moved several times trying to start a crop on other people's land. James did some preaching and taught school to help us get by, but times never got better. Even with a decent crop, after we paid for the use of the land, there was little left. It seemed like there was always another mouth to feed. We read the Bible every night, and we prayed and prayed. James had read a flyer he found in town, and he was sure that our future would be better in a new place with lots of promise. No more tenant farming for us. He managed to downplay the facts that we were going into Indian Territory with no laws, red dirt, and not a lot of trees.

In Texas, our homes were made of wood and were small, but adequate even for our ever-expanding family. We didn't own them, but we were grateful for the shelter. The houses kept us dry and safe while we worked the land. I had friends to talk with, learn from, and share dreams with. We left a little later than we had planned, but with no serious delays, we would be there on time. It had to work out for us because we had nowhere else to go.

As we neared what I was told was the Oklahoma border, we forged a dangerous river with little loss even though many of our belongings got wet, I was able to keep the cornmeal dry. The land on the other side looked less friendly than I had even imagined. Dry dirt, scruffy trees—how would we ever survive? James was still so enthusiastic, and the boys were too while I sat quietly and prayed. I was told our new home would be made of mud, not wood. How would I keep a mud house clean? I found comfort that so many other families and individuals were close by, all of us on the same journey. Thousands of people were coming from the west, the north, the east as well as those of us from the south.

We were camped just a few miles from the starting line that had been laid out by the Federal Government. Our journey had few disruptions, and we arrived two days before April 22. We chose a small clearing in which to camp. People were crowding us, but we stood our ground. James decided he would have a better chance of getting a good claim if he left our wagon and went on horseback with our oldest son. He left me with the other boys, and since we had a loaded wagon, he left our rifle for protection. Early in the morning that Monday, we said a prayer, kissed goodbye, and he and Risdon were off.

A short time after they left, I could feel the ground shake like thunder from the stampede of horses, carriages, and people running on foot. We heard cannon fire, gunshots, and shouts at noon, the start of the land rush. It was all very scary to me, but I was busy keeping the boys from running amuck. James had read all the rules and knew exactly what to do. I knew it would be late at night or even the next day before they returned. The claims were staked out, and homesteaders left something significant on their desired claim while they left to register.

Risdon, who was tall for his age and looked like a man, was left at our claim, hoping no one would challenge him. Homesteaders were required to register with the Federal Land Office that was set up in tents. I remember my husband telling me that he was surprised at how many folks couldn't read or write. He helped a few make their claims. There were fights and gun shots, but the worst part was that some of the settlers had breached the borders. They were first to make claims on the best land that they had already started improving to assure that they would retain it. They came to be known as Sooners and were ostracized within our new community.

Miraculously, James and Risdon returned almost at dawn with a duly recorded claim! Some of our new traveling friends had also managed to procure land, but with plots of 160 acres, I wondered if we would ever see them again. We knew of only one family traveling with us that was denied a claim. They were denied because the father had fought on the Confederate side of the Civil War.

The next couple of days we drove on in our wagon to find our stake. All of our spirits were high, even mine, although I was already dealing with the red dirt that stuck to everything. James had planned that we would live in our wagon and tent until he and the boys built our home. It was almost May and I began to see wildflowers popping up just as they had in Texas, and I was hopeful when I thought of picking them and putting them in a jar on a table in our new home. As we approached our land, I saw some sod houses started by the Sooners. They looked dreadful, and I feared it would take more than wildflowers to make a home.

James assured me once again that we had brought tools and sons, which except for prayers is all we need. Grateful to stay in one place, now I had to figure out how to feed everyone. There was water, but not very close so I took the wagon, my youngest son, James, and the rifle. Our plan was to find it and bring back as much as possible. I was very stoic so as not to worry James. He was watching for Indians, and I think he was more excited at the prospect of seeing them than not. On the way here, my husband had talked to other settlers about how to build a "home" from the earth before winter. It only took three months to complete our first Oklahoma home.

"Soddy" 1890

I had brought my iron stove, and it was the first thing I moved into our new home. It was summer, and the wildflowers were gone, so the stove represented a real home to me, and I could prepare our meals. The cornmeal supply that we brought was dwindling. Everyone was tired of cornbread and grits, but also grateful we had food. My husband and sons were good hunters so we occasionally had the bounty of prairie chickens, rabbits, and whatever else they could track. In the summer and early fall, I continued to cook outside over the campfire. It was more pleasant for me and kept the smoke out of our house. My fears about how to keep our house clean were made real as I struggled to make a home; I never stopped trying to sweep.

Some settlers brought furniture, but we made our own from salvaged or traded lumber. I made all our clothes by hand as I had in Texas. I used old flour sacks and tent material for shirts and pants. By the time they were handed down to the youngest there were more patches than fabric. During the day, the older boys worked the land and Little James helped me with my chores. At night, we read the Bible, and James taught all the boys how to read and write. He wanted them to have farming skills, but he felt that the key to their future was education. When the schools were founded in the next couple of years, the boys were ready! That is how we spent our first winter, and it was brutal. At least the cold weather killed most of the bugs burrowing in the sod of our home. We were low on food and spent a good deal of time looking for things to burn to stay warm. As spring approached, and I could once again enjoy the wildflowers, I had renewed hope. We survived, had a winter wheat crop, and I even planted a small kitchen garden when the frost thawed.

I was enjoying some support from our new neighbors, and I was feeling new life in my belly. On an early June day, several of our neighbors gathered and shared our meager stores to have a celebration. Someone brought a fiddle and there was music and dancing. I had forgotten how much fun James and I could have with each other. His long lanky arm's flailed about in rhythm to the music. It made me laugh and brought on that familiar warm feeling. The boys had never seen such a sight.

The concerns about the Indians were never realized, and we rarely saw them. The seeds for our next corn crop were given to us by the railroad. The town of McMillan, in Chickasaw Nation, sprouted as a result of the land rush. It was a big event for us to take our wagon into town and socialize a bit.

We continued to make friends with our land. We suffered a drought that summer, and I had to go farther for water. We were blessed to have a cow and God knew I was grateful for the animal, even though I was never sure of how James acquired it. We slowly became one with our land,

and my belly grew with the added hope and promise of a new life for our family. As November approached, we were better prepared than last winter, but still in our "soddy" as we called our mud home.

As my time neared, a neighbor came to help me deliver my baby. The whole family was sure it would be a boy, and we had all agreed on another boy name. My last push delivered my precious miracle. A beautiful healthy baby girl with slate blue eyes and a little reddish fuzz on her head. Born on Sunday, November 16, 1890, I named her after me and my mother, Amanda Melvina Knight. I have always been called Melviney, and I will call her Vina. My mother had told me that our name meant beauty and strength. Vina already had the beauty, and I prayed for her strength. I was so endeared to this child who came from my body amidst infinite struggles, and I prayed that her life would be better than mine.

All the family was so excited to welcome a baby girl. Risdon, now fifteen, and almost grown, was the most smitten with his little sister. Risdon became her companion, and after all day in the fields, he rushed home to play and cuddle with Vina before her bedtime. He made little toys for her and could always make her smile and laugh.

I only knew this lovely child for thirteen months. Our third Oklahoma winter was treacherous. Lots of illness, damaged crops, but we were slowly moving towards a brighter future. Shortly after Vina's first birthday, I became ill. I managed to keep the household together with the help of the younger boys, but after a month, I couldn't get out of bed. There was ice everywhere outside, but I felt like I was on fire. I coughed and wheezed, even with herbs and tea brought by neighbors, I knew I was nearing my death. I wasn't fearful for myself, but very fearful for those left behind. I regretfully said goodbye to my beloved husband, sons, and precious daughter. I remember James praying over me, and the boys crying and praying. I was mostly delirious, seeing visions of my long-departed parents and buried baby boys. In a conscious moment, I remember seeing Risdon on the floor on a blanket in front of our stove playing with Vina and a doll I had made for her. It gave me peace as I drew my last breath on this earth, to know that he would always be her protector. Vina's giggle was the last earthly sound I heard.

Risdon Daniel Knight, 1876-1912

CHAPTER TWO

Risdon Daniel Knight

I remember how our home smelled that day. A blend of dirt, corn grits, and smoke with a bit of lavender that Mama had dried last summer. It smelled that way most days, but today there was a different kind of smell, the smell of intense sorrow. My whole family gathered in silence. Everyone had spoken all of their words. Cried all of their tears. My mother was dying, and I thought that by not saying anything, it might not happen. It was shortly after Christmas that she took ill and probably days before any of us noticed. Finally, one day she left her chores undone and took to her bed. A few days more of her coughing and making deep sounds in her chest, and I knew she was really sick. Occasionally she opened her eyes to look at us, but she could barely speak.

Father wouldn't let us get close to her for fear we would get ill too. He brought her broth and read the Bible to her. That day, I was sitting on the floor in front of the stove with Vina. We played with the doll Mama made for her, and I was trying to make her laugh. I caught my mother's eye, and a sweet look came upon her face. She closed her eyes and slipped away from our family forever. I held tight to Vina as I saw a tear in the eye of my father. A sight I would not see for another fifteen years.

I'm not sure how the news spread, but two neighbor ladies came and washed my mother's body and dressed her in her only nice dress. Father made a plain wood coffin from lumber collected and salvaged from neighbors. Thomas and I dug her grave. Father had chosen a spot on our property under a tree. The land that had fought so hard against us yielded easily to preparations for Mama's eternal rest. Our home was too small for an appropriate wake, but our father with his proper Reverend voice performed a committal service at her grave while holding her Bible. Gratefully, Vina was unaware of the event. I remember thinking that seeing my father standing straight in his one suit, hair and mustache trimmed and combed, hatless, and committing his beloved wife to the Lord, may have been his finest moment.

After Mama died, our family still struggled to get a foothold in that unwelcoming land. Fortunately, that spring brought good farming weather. Father, Thomas, Bolivar, and even Little James and I toiled to expand our corn crop and reap the winter wheat. While my darling Vina brought much joy to our family, there were practical issues to solve. The younger boys learned to grind cornmeal, prepare meals, clean our clothes, feed the chickens, and haul water. One of us always had to stay home during the day to take care of the baby. Father never complained, but the situation took a huge toll on our mostly self-sufficient family.

A barren woman on a neighboring farm offered father a solution. He agreed to allow Mrs. Moshaw and her husband take care of the baby during the day, and Vina would occasionally spend the night. We all missed her a lot. Even though it wasn't every day, it felt to me that she was gone more than she was with us. I was allowed to be the one to take Vina to our neighbors and pick her up. It was the best part of my day. I rode horseback on Jessie, our trusted horse, and kept Vina tucked safely in my lap. She loved it when we galloped, and she was always such a joyful baby. We realized the importance of the whole family working on our farm. We all understood that as she got older, she would be home again every day, and she could start to take over the chores of our mother. But until then, we relied on the Moshaws to care for her. When the next crop came in, father arranged for Vina to stay with the trusted neighbors for a couple of days, the longest she'd been away.

I rode over to pick up Vina in the late afternoon of the third day. As I approached their home, I immediately sensed something was wrong. To my horror, everything was totally quiet, and I feared the worst...maybe an Indian attack. I didn't even knock, just went forcefully inside. The house was totally empty. Nothing, no furniture, no tools, no chickens in the yard. And no bodies, dead or alive. The place was completely silent, like no one had ever lived there. Deep ruts in the dirt immediately led me to believe our trusted neighbors had loaded up their substantial wagon, along with my beloved sister, and fled! I mounted Jessie and rode as fast as I could, hollering for my father all the way.

Hearing me approach, everyone met me outside of our "soddy," just as the sun was setting. "She's gone! she's gone!" I yelled. "They've stolen Vina! Let's go after them NOW!" I saw absolutely no reason why we couldn't leave right now. I was astounded when father didn't agree.

My father, James Knight, was an even tempered man. Having always considered himself to be a preacher, he was usually able to look at all sides of a situation, make a decision, and at least in our household convince everyone he was right. If that didn't work, he just reminded us who was the head of our family. Many arguments in the past had taught all of us that it was futile to try to express our feelings on any important matter. It was God's way and father's way, and often they didn't always agree. It was sometimes a toss-up as to which one came out on top.

Father explained that there was no law in this territory and no one we could get to help us. We had no idea of the head start they had, and we would lose the wheel tracks in the red dirt after a few miles. We would go riding off into the land that we know nothing about except that it is full of Indians. Not all of the tribes were satisfied with the latest treaty, and some settlers were afraid of violence. After the decision was made not to follow my kidnapped sister, I was still riled up, and father surprisingly let me have my say. "I vow that I will find my sister one day. Before I marry, I will tell my wife that when I find my sister, she will live with us, and I will take care of her!"

We continued to work the farm, but the joy had gone out of our home, at least for me. Father had been making the trip into town more often and subsidizing our meager farming with teaching and preaching. He remarried a couple of years after my mother died, and both Thomas and I thought it was a sign for us to leave. Shortly after moving into town, we both got jobs. I married Emma Pruitt, who quickly agreed to my terms of marriage about Vina. After trying a couple of other jobs, I became an insurance salesman. With my way of talking to folks, the selling part was easy, and I made a good living for my family without having dirt under my fingernails. Part of the attraction of my job was that I would be traveling to Arkansas, Texas, and Louisiana, places I might one day find my sister. We had our first baby, Maudie May, in 1898. I adored that baby girl, but she awakened all of my deep feelings for Vina.

James Jefferson Knight, 1852-1918

CHAPTER THREE

James Jefferson Knight

Almighty God, have you forsaken me? You led us on this journey to find a new life. You kept us safe against all odds. I prayed and honored you. I spread your Holy word. I married a beautiful God-fearing woman who bore me seven children. We toiled the land you provided and survived harsh winters and drought. You blessed me with a precious daughter but took away my beloved wife. Please dearest Lord, forgive me for the dreadful decision I have made. I am on my knees dear Lord, please hear my prayer of desperation.

The loss of Melviney devastated my world. We married with such joy and faith in the future. I met her when she was only twelve, seven years younger than me. Such a lighthearted, joyful little flower she was. I teased her a bit, but we were just friends for many years until our relationship changed. At fifteen, she began to look at me in a different way and was very open to my affection. We had fun, we danced even when we had to make our own music. Our marriage was performed in 1874 by a friend of mine who was also a minister.

Melviney came from a family of farmers, and we found a small tenant farm with a house to start our family in Sulfur Springs, Texas. Our first son, Risdon, was born two years later. God was good to us, but still we struggled. Our second son, Moody, was born and lived less than a year.

Melviney prepared his body for burial and wept for days. Perhaps this isn't the place for us, I thought, so I asked for God's guidance, and a short time later, we moved to a more promising farm, this one in Cook County. Folks were friendlier and more encouraging here. I even did a little preaching from our front porch. Melviney's spirits improved, and our first crop allowed me to barter for a used iron stove. My wife was so happy and on that very day, she told me that our family was expanding. Thomas Jefferson was born and to our delight God brought us another strong healthy son.

Two more moves and two more tenant farms, and two more sons were born, Boliver and James. I felt a desperate need to find a way to make a better life. If I had had more money, I probably would have started drinking regularly, and I had to ask forgiveness from God for the times I shared alcohol with other men. Sorrow overcame me as I watched our circumstances slowly drain the joy from my beautiful wife. Another son, Benjamin, was born and only lived two months. Melviney was a wonderful mother and very creative about making our homes, but she was again heartbroken at losing a child. What we both lost at that time was hope.

I went into town trying to find a job or anything I could do for money. An East Texas windstorm blew in, sending garbage and dirt flying in the street. My boot stepped on a dirty, yellowed torn piece of paper. It was an advertisement for the Oklahoma Land Rush, to be held in six months. Land was to be given away to those who staked a claim! This must be our sign from God! The answer to our prayers! Glory be to God! I got home as fast as I could to share the news. We would actually own our land! Our hard work would pay off. My wife and I began to dream again…and plan… oh my, how we planned!! We had a wagon and two horses because of our many moves. There was time for one more good crop that would allow us the money to gather the rest of the supplies we needed. We had new goals and were certain that God was on our side.

We were in Grice, Texas, and had lived there the longest of any place. The planting season was upon us, and this time in addition to corn and sugar cane, we planted cotton. It was our first really good crop, and even the little ones could help us pick it for market. Neighbors helped each other, and we paid our land lease and had some left over. We all worked day and night preparing for our journey to the promise of a new and better life in Oklahoma. Our possessions were meager, but I was determined that with God's help we could make it. Any doubts I had I kept to myself. I sensed that my wife wasn't sure, but she never voiced her concerns. I always bore my responsibilities as head of my household with pride. The boys were not to question, rules can't be broken, respect your mother, do God's work, always. I admit to questioning and sometimes turning away from God... but I always got back on track. I spent a lot of time talking to neighbors, and a few were also heading to Oklahoma. We had a Winchester rifle for protection. It was old, inherited from Melviney's father and a relic from the Civil War, but it worked. I had handled guns my whole life. It became even more real to me that I needed to teach my wife how to shoot to protect herself and the boys. That rifle probably wouldn't scare any Indians, but having it made me feel better.

As the time neared, I felt that Melviney didn't question my resolve which enabled me to keep my pride intact when sometimes it was all I had. The wagon was packed, and the journey started. On pure faith with help from other travelers and the uplifting spirit of my wife, we made it to the promised land and staked our claim!

Building a shelter was our first project. Our sod house had to be at least twelve feet by fourteen feet to realize the claim. Cutting the sod itself was more difficult than I had imagined. I brought a few tools, but only my machete was able to cut through the massive roots. I was told it was best to cut the sod in triangles to help reinforce the walls. As soon as we cut a block, we had to use it so it would attach itself to the block next to it. It took three months to complete, with two windows and a door. Melviney moved in her treasured stove, and it was home.

Life got better for the homesteaders. A post office was established in 1892 in nearby McMillan, but the area was still considered Cheyenne Territory and Chickasaw Nation. Cotton had become a major crop, but we stuck to corn and wheat. Schools were established, and all the boys were eager to attend, or at least preferred it to farm chores. Unsurprisingly, the chores were still there when they got home.

Two years after Melviney died, I married a lady named Faythe Ann. She was young and strong, the daughter of another minister I had met. She taught school but was happy to move into our home and share my bed. There was a pleasantness about her that I enjoyed.

By this time, building materials were available, and churches were being established. At the five-year mark, homesteaders could officially own their land if they had lived on it, improved it, and made it productive with crops or livestock. Farmers had more help with crops and supplies were plentiful, for a price.

And I had one more son.

As my boys got older and attended school, one by one they chose to leave the farm. Risdon had been antsy ever since his mother died, and I could feel that Thomas was probably right behind him. Thomas decided that he would use his middle name, so we started calling him Jeff. Risdon moved into town and tried several jobs. He had a salesman's personality, and he settled on insurance; he even tried to sell me a policy. It was a little too late for me.

Risdon married Emma Florence Pruitt, who had quickly agreed to his terms of the marriage. When he found his sister, she could come to live with them. He and Emma had a total of six children. The first was

Maudie May in 1898. Jeff married Sarah Melinda Pruitt, Emma's sister, that same year. They had a total of eleven children, of which I only knew four. Bolivar left as soon as he could and married Malinda Kesterson in 1900, and as far as I know only had one child. James married Lonnie Sanders (Annie).

I was aware that Risdon continued to search for his baby sister. He made a good living, but his job required lots of traveling. I knew he looked for her wherever he went, but I tried not to think about her at all. The pain of not having her in my life was too connected to losing my wife. After fourteen years, I was astonished when he came bounding into my house with the news that he had found her!

PART TWO

CHAPTER FOUR

The Search for Vina

In 1901, Frisco Railroad and others were constructed all over Oklahoma, making it feasible to efficiently move wheat, cotton, and grain from farms to markets. Oklahoma was starting to thrive. As life improved, the railroads also started carrying passengers, building larger stations and nicer passenger cars. Railroad stations became a social hub for salesmen, farmers, cowboys, and businessmen with goods to sell. There was usually a game of checkers, discussions of politics, gossip, and cigars. The trains mostly ran on time, but occasionally tempers would flare, and fights would break out. This was Risdon's life when he was on the road selling insurance.

Risdon was quite charming and eased into conversations. As he traveled, he told the same story to anyone who would listen, of his quest to find his kidnapped sister, always remembering to give her updated age and what he imagined to be her current appearance. He included her slate gray/blue eyes and auburn hair. He and his brothers were over six feet, so he assumed that she was tall as well. He couldn't hide the emotion in his voice as he told the story, and the pain of his loss was always with him. The many repetitious stories he told in various stations were usually met with, "Sorry sir, tough circumstances, I really wish I could help you. Good luck finding your sister."

Until one day in April, 1906, in a small railroad station in Texas, Risdon told his story once again, remembering to update her age, now to fifteen. He hadn't lost his resolve, but he was allowing a bit of doubt to sneak in from time to time. On this unusually cool spring day, he experienced the same scenario and same response from the travelers gathered around the iron stove. But as he was heading out to catch his train, a man leaning up against a wall smoking a cigar gestured to him. "I heard your story, sir," he said. "This is a long shot, but I'm from Vivian, Louisiana. My daughter is sixteen, and she has a friend named Miss Pledger, who I think could be your sister. I don't know her eye color or age, but she is tall and has incredibly beautiful red hair.

Risdon literally stopped in his tracks, gathered as much information as he could from the gentleman, and bought a ticket to Louisiana. Since Vivian was such a small town, he had no doubt that he could find Miss Pledger and see if, indeed, she was his sister. He didn't let the different last name deter him. After all it had been fourteen years since she was taken from his family. The name of the couple whose empty house he visited was Moshaw. He would never forget that name, but he had never run into anyone else with that name in Texas, Arkansas, Oklahoma, or Louisiana. Perhaps they changed it. Who knows, but he was soon going to find out! He tried hard not to get his hopes up, but the train ride seemed endless. He changed trains in Shreveport, a town he visited often and where he probably could have sold some policies today, but he was on a determined mission.

Arriving in Vivian in the early afternoon, once again he talked to a few citizens in the train station and settled on visiting a house on Forest St. His walk to the nearby home calmed his nerves. Even though Vivian was a lovely small town, in his distraction he didn't see the redbuds starting to bloom or the picturesque downtown. He stopped in front of a neatly kept white Victorian house with an impressive front porch. If this was Vina's home, it gave him comfort to know she was obviously well cared for.

Risdon adjusted his coat, tie, and hat, and straightened to his full six-foot one inch height. Although his heart was pounding, he was self-assured and knew he was doing the right thing. Opening the gate of the fence, he must have made an impressive presence as he walked up the path. Holding to his resolve, he strode up the steps to the front door and knocked. Through the screen door he could see the woman walking toward him to answer his knock, and his heart stood still for a moment. He recognized her! It was Blanche Moshaw!

She, however, didn't recognize the handsome well-dressed man at her door as he had been just a teenager when she saw him last. His smile showed under his mustache, and he said he had news for her. He was charming, and she was curious, so she invited him into her home directing him to a seat in the parlor, furnished with a pipe organ and Victorian furniture. Blanche was alone; she told him her husband was at work and her daughter at school. She was very gracious, and then he introduced himself. Risdon watched her face grow ashen as she grasped the news he had for her.

She had been found out.

For fourteen years, Blanche Moshaw Pledger had covered her tracks, or so she thought. She had left Oklahoma in the dead of night, taking everything she and her husband possessed, as well as a tiny baby that wasn't theirs. Oklahoma farming hadn't turned out well for them, and she had not been able to conceive a child she so desperately wanted. She justified their actions that night as yet another opportunity to start over.

Starting over was familiar to her. She and her husband had no family to anchor them and had left a failing farm in Tennessee in the hope of obtaining land and starting a family in Oklahoma. Both were anxious for a new opportunity, and she had enough money to fund their journey. But she had not been able to conceive a child and she was as barren as the Oklahoma land. When a neighboring family, the Knights, lost their mother to consumption, she saw a different kind of opportunity. Knowing the hardships the Knights would face without a mother to care for the tiny child, she offered to help care for the baby. Blanche quickly became totally obsessed by her love and need for this child, crying every night after the family's oldest son, Risdon, would come to pick her up. Feeling as though her own child was ripped from her arms, she told herself that she would be a good mother to little Vina, better than no mother at all because she could give her undivided attention, loving her and caring for her better than anyone.

Blanche's husband Michael was a bit lazy and easily manipulated. It was not difficult for her to convince him of her plan. He was happy to get out of Oklahoma--farming was a lot harder than any of the many jobs he had. She surmised that the Knight family already had so many children, and the father, James, needed all of them to help with the farm, surely, they wouldn't follow them. And so, the Moshaw family left their homestead in the dead of night under a dark sky, heading east and hoping they wouldn't be followed.

To outward appearance, they were a typical little family looking for a new place to live. Blanche Moshaw was surprised at how kind and helpful everyone was when they saw their precious baby girl. They had breakdowns and weather delays, and even had to sell some of their belongings along the way. They had no real plan other than to get as far away from Oklahoma as possible. They settled in a logging town in Arkansas and moved into a company supplied house. Michael took a job at the sawmill, and Blanche spent her days with Vina. She made beautiful dresses for her and loved combing her thick shiny, curly, auburn hair that she loosely tied with a ribbon, a fashion of that age. She shopped with many peddlers, looking for perfect ribbons for Vina's hair. Blanche basked in the many compliments about her daughter's hair. "She inherited the color from my grandmother," she would always say. She taught Vina manners and to read and write. By the time Vina could go to the newly established one room school, Vina was ready and eager to learn.

One tragic day in 1897, Mr. Moshaw was killed in a logging accident at the mill. Left alone, the widow and her young daughter were treated well by the community. Vina grieved for her father and even though she was only seven years old, she immersed herself in books and anything she could find to read. But as kind as the community was, Blanche didn't want to live on charity, and left with Vina, once again starting over.

Blanche took her daughter to a new home in Texas and then to Louisiana, where she met a tall, burly red-headed Irishman named Arthur Pledger. He was a prospering tool-pusher in the oil patches of Northern Louisiana, an area that quickly became a hub of commerce and activity, especially in nearby Shreveport. Arthur was younger than Blanche and susceptible to her charms. Blanche was a wonderful cook, and Arthur Pledger loved to eat. Never having had children, he quickly became enthralled with the quiet, shy eight-year-old Vina. In 1889, he and Blanche married, and his prosperity allowed Blanche the life she wanted for herself and her daughter.

Arthur was flattered when Blanche asked him if he would allow Vina to have his last name. He never suspected he was part of a ruse: with a red-head Irish husband and a new name, Blanche felt certain now that no one would ever find them "They probably didn't bother to follow us anyway!" Blanche often said to herself. Vina thrived in school and had a few friends, but her mother socialized more than ever while Vina mostly kept to herself, living the lives she found in her books. This gentile life was idyllic until Risdon Knight knocked on her door.

Back to Forest Street that spring day in 1906. After introducing himself,

Risdon controlled the conversation, assuring Blanche he wasn't there to cause trouble. Vina would be home from school soon, and he wanted to know all about her life for the last fourteen years. Blanch described her as a bit shy, often retreating to the company of her books. She was a good student and oftentimes was bored by her lessons. As a teenager, she had become more outgoing with a few girl friends that spent time together, mostly giggling and planning for whatever is to come. Vina didn't make quick decisions but is resolute in what she decides. According to Blanche, she was always pleasant to share time with, was a good conversationalist, and often had strong opinions.

When Vina came through the door after school, she stopped short when she saw a stranger in the parlor. Risdon knew her immediately, her abundant red hair piled loosely on her head, her deep-set eyes like their father's, her tall stature, and shy but charming smile. He assured himself that the mention of her red hair in his descriptions to strangers was what led him to her. He arose when she entered and could hardly stay seated after he sat back in the chair. Every part of his being wanted to jump up and hug her and dance with joy. He sensed that his enthusiasm would scare her. Until this moment, he had never thought about how this discovery would impact her life.

Forest Street, Vivian, Louisiana

Blanche Pledger, 1868-1935

Vina, 1893

Vina, 1896

CHAPTER FIVE

Amanda Melvina Knight Pledger

Diary entry: April 14, 1916

My whole life is a lie! Today, after coming home from school to a stranger in the parlor, my whole life changed! My mother is not my mother! My mother is dead! My stepfather, who I thought was my father is dead, and my real father is alive! I thought I was an only child and now I'm told that I have four brothers, one stepbrother and a multitude of cousins, all who live but a train ride away! My oldest brother is sitting in front of me! Strangely, I did feel an instant familiarity with him. But I think that if I were to read this experience in a book, I would be very skeptical.

Risdon stayed for dinner and met Arthur Pledger. I don't remember "mother", at least the only mother I've ever known, soliciting Arthur's opinion in the parlor, but his opinion wouldn't have mattered anyway. After a while, I began to comprehend what had happened and to understand how, but not why, I was deceived.

Overwhelming for a person who, only a few hours ago thought I was an only child. My emotions are like a whirlwind with no place to go and agitated further by being told what my mother and brother had decided for me. I am almost sixteen years old. School will be out for the summer in less than two months. I will travel to Oklahoma to meet my father, my brothers, my sisters-in-law. and cousins. I will stay with Risdon and his family. What will become of me?

Arthur and Vina had both been deceived. As rough and surly as he appeared, Arthur was always gentle with Vina, and she was proud to introduce him as her father. Of course, she knew he wasn't her real father, but he had filled that role in her life. He had a jovial side that helped to balance the sternness of her "mother". At this moment, she looked to him for support.

After making plans with Blanche for Vina's trip, Risdon returned home to Oklahoma to share the news that he had found their sister! Those first few days after his visit were a bit of a blur. Vina remembered going to school, and that their routines remained the same. When she heard her parents arguing rather loudly one night, she buried her head in a book, but no one spoke of that fateful afternoon.

Once the secrets and lies were brought to the surface, everything changed. Vina was glad to go to school, but not so glad to return home. She spent most of her time in her beautiful bedroom. She and Blanche had recently changed it to more of a young lady's bedroom, with a pink bedspread and curtains that they shopped for on one of their Shreveport outings. Arthur had freshly painted the room and her bookshelves, and she took great pleasure in positioning each book in the perfect place. There was a dressing table with a mirror that had been ordered from a catalog, which she also used for a desk. She made her own bed every morning, but Blanche kept the pillows and sheets always fresh. She had a Negro woman, Miss Audie, that helped her with the housework, but Blanche did all the cooking.

Vina kept the news to herself and found solace in her bedroom. She brooded on her life and her story. She wondered about the woman who had given birth to her, her real mother who gave her her name, Amanda Melvina

Knight. She loved the only mother she knew, but she wondered what her other life would have been like. She finally confided in her best friend, Fiona. Shockingly, Fiona had said that her father had asked her if she'd been visited by a man from Oklahoma. When she heard herself telling the story, Vina was surprised at how much emotion it brought up. She hadn't used the word before, but she realized that she'd been kidnapped! Emotions roiled through her—betrayal, anger, and immense sadness. Since her parents never talked about it and acted like it never happened, at least now she had someone with whom to share her dilemmas. It was during this time that she, Amanda Melvina Knight Pledger, realized that there was no one in the world that she could totally trust, and she promised to never allow herself to be put in a position to have to completely rely on someone else.

Vina soon started to look forward to her upcoming summer adventure in Oklahoma. This would be a very different summer than she'd ever known. Past summers were spent leisurely with a few girlfriends, having picnics, playing card games, and an occasional train ride to Shreveport. She didn't even have a suitcase, but one miraculously appeared, and her mother helped her pack. They even went into Shreveport and shopped for a couple of new blouses and a skirt. Her favorite blouse was an off-white linen. It was soft, stylish with a high neck, lots of lace trim, tiny pleats in the front, and puffy long sleeves, and gave her confidence as soon as she tried it on. The second blouse was simpler, with a soft bow at the neck. She chose a black skirt because she was warned about all the red dirt. After all the usual end of school activities, she was ready to go. Her classmates rarely left town for more than a few days, and she thought most secretly envied her. But no one, other than Fiona, was aware of why she was traveling to Oklahoma.

It was time to go to the train station. She had been there many times, but it was exciting to have a new destination. She wore a practical suit for traveling, and her mother gave her a small basket of food for the journey.

Arthur gave her a big hug, but "mother" said only, "Remember dear, they aren't like us."

Vina had never traveled alone, and welcomed her newfound independence. Arthur had given her some tips on how to behave toward passengers and how to change trains. The basket she brought on the train was full with two books to read, including a new treasured poetry book, some paper and a pencil as she was thinking about writing some poems herself. The train ride was enjoyable with the gentle swaying movement. On short train trips, she hadn't noticed that the seats were only slightly padded and not very comfortable. There were more stops than she'd expected, but she found the activity of people at the station exciting. There were some very unruly children on the train, and she thought to herself that Blanche would fix that.

Reading on the train was more difficult than she had expected because of her many thoughts and anticipation of what lay ahead. Because she had felt very comfortable around Risdon, even after such a short time, she had let him hug her as he left and now felt reassured that everything would work out. They'd been exchanging post cards for the past two months, and her brother had written down the names of all her new family members so she could learn them and not be overwhelmed. Vina sat by the window so she could see when the landscape started to change, as mother had described Oklahoma as mostly uncivilized with lots of red dirt, very dry, and very hot, and it isn't even a state yet, she'd added. There are Indians, cowboys, guns and lawlessness. All of the things meant to deter her, instead piqued her interest. A few passengers sat next to her, but after a greeting, she discouraged further conversation by appearing to read her book. Out of the window she saw mostly farmland and rolling hills, and everything appeared quite civilized. Whatever she experienced, it was just a visit, after all, she reminded herself. She would be going home again if she so chose.

The last thing Risdon had said to her before he left was that the decision of where to live was hers to make.

CHAPTER SIX

The Return to Oklahoma

A slight curve in the tracks allowed Vina to see a glimpse of the train station at her final stop. It was a small wooden structure with a few people milling about. As the train chugged into the station, Vina immediately recognized the tallest man on the platform. Risdon was there, as promised, waving his hat and smiling, surrounded by his wife and four children. As Vina stepped down off the train, her brother grabbed her suitcase, and she was met with hugs and warm greetings from his wife Emma. The children yelled, "Auntie, Auntie." It took a moment for Vina to realize she was the Auntie. Risdon had brought a buggy, and they loaded up and were on their way to meet Vina's real father. The buggy was crowded, and she was unaccustomed to having children on her lap, but she felt a lot of love in this crammed space.

Vina had not expected to see such an old man. He was tall, but a bit stooped from his fifty-five years of hard work, had rough calloused hands, thinning white hair and mustache, but his smile was big when he instantly arose to hold his daughter in his arms. She was overwhelmed with emotion and tears, feeling an instant connection to this man. At least three times he released his hug, held her at arm's length to study her face, and then pulled her toward him again. She noticed he had the same unique slate gray eye color as hers, and she saw a tear in his. He had remarried two years after her mother died, and she met her stepmother, Faythe, who seemed very concerned about him. Vina was hoping for time alone with her father so she could ask questions about her mother. But that would have to wait.

Risdon gathered everyone back in the buggy to go to his and Emma's home. When there, Vina was shown where she would sleep, sharing a room and bed with eight-year-old Maudie May. Dorothy, aged three, was also in the room. They had a simple dinner, and Vina was exhausted, so off to bed they went. The sheets with a slight familiar scent of lavender were soft and wrinkled but comfortable. She had never shared a bed with anyone but didn't have time to think about it before she was fast asleep. During subsequent nights, there was giggly sister talk that she found comforting and surprisingly enjoyed. Vina had spent every night of her life that she could remember by herself, in her own room on starched stretched sheets in total dark silence.

Everyone got up early, and Vina was told there was going to be a picnic to meet folks and celebrate her arrival. Choosing a summer dress with small white flowers and a white sweater, she didn't really think she would need the sweater but was aware that the dress accentuated her expanding chest, and she didn't want anyone looking at her. At least not that part of her. With her long hair piled on her head as was the style in Vivian, she was ready for the day.

Tables were set up with cloths and lots of fresh food, cookies, and cake. Vina tried to help with the preparations, but everyone seemed delighted to meet her, and she was barraged with hugs and questions about her life. She was surrounded by multitudes of brothers, sisters-in-law, nieces, nephews, and cousins. All related to her and all bearing the same last name...her name, KNIGHT.

That night when Maudie May was finally asleep, and the house was quiet, or at least as quiet as it got, Vina reflected on the day. After a few days, she had adjusted to her place in the family. She was in between age groups, the sisters-in-laws were nice to her but couldn't relate to her other world. Their interests were their children, their homes, and their husbands, mostly in that order. The children were playful and fun and even in her summer dresses, Vina found herself enjoying running and playing. She even took off her shoes and ran barefooted with them. Her "mother" would have been horrified. Maybe that's why it was so much fun, she thought. The children all loved it when Auntie read books to them and helped to make up silly poems. She taught them card games that she'd played with her friends.

A couple of weeks into her visit, Risdon had arranged for a studio photograph to be taken of the five siblings. She knew exactly what she wanted to wear—the new black skirt and her favorite linen blouse with the high neck and puffy sleeves and her usual hair style. Her four brothers were in their best clothes too, and each one looked so very handsome. The photographer instructed them to not even move a muscle. Feeling such joy made the requirement of holding still during the process almost impossible, and a little smile escaped her face.

She grew close to Maudie and forged a bond that lasted the rest of their lives, even with eight years difference in their ages. Still, she longed for some time alone with her father, and finally, toward the end of her stay, it happened. Her father took her to her mother's grave where the only marker was a wooden one, that he replaced frequently. He described their courtship and how much fun they always had. Melviney was only fifteen, Vina's age, when they'd married, and he was twenty-two. They grew up near each other, and he had seen her many years before and was attracted to her spirit. She was beautiful, strong, and loving. He mentioned how she found joy in such simple things...wildflowers, sunsets, wild birds. She had fiercely loved her family, but with the death of their two boys, a little bit of her died also. Describing their hardships and many moves, he told Vina that her mother always created a warm, loving home no matter where they were. Melviney bore him seven children, and Vina needed no reminder that she was his only daughter and the last of the children he and Melviney had together.

He looked incredibly sad when he spoke of the years he and Vina hadn't shared. He looked straight into her eyes when he asked for reassurance that she'd had a good life. His look was piercing, and she felt it in her soul. He told her of the joy her parents shared at the birth of their baby girl. Her mother loved her with all of her being and prayed that Vina's life would be easier than hers had been. He gave her a picture of her mother and her mother's Bible, a gift that would tie her to her mother forever. The scriptures she would read had perhaps been also read by her mother years before, and a calming peace suddenly surrounded Vina, her mother's namesake.

When it was nearing fall and time for Vina to go home, she found she had mixed emotions. She knew she could stay. Never had she been surrounded with so much love. "Mother" or Blanche, was right. They aren't like us ... they don't hide under pretenses or use fancy words to make them feel important. They don't seem concerned about what others think, and they don't harbor secrets and lies. They appreciate every possession and work hard and share with others. They show love for each other openly and freely. Vina also felt closer to God in Oklahoma.

These thoughts both angered and disturbed her. She could never again call Blanche her mother, but she could go back to Vivian where she wanted to finish out her last year of school and see friends. She left some of her books for other family members and took the most precious one, her mother's Bible, with her. She was always generous with sharing her books, but wrote in each one, "My books are my friends, and I like to keep them close." This sentiment was meant to remind borrowers to reunite her with her books. She was sad to leave her family and asked to come back the next summer.

Oklahoma Reunion, 1906 — Bolivar, Vina, James, Risdon, Jeff

James Jefferson Knight, Vina's father 1906

CHAPTER SEVEN

Amanda Melvina Knight

Look to the Future

Vina went back to Louisiana. This time the train ride seemed much shorter than her previous one. She had a new identity. She had tangible items proving who she was, and pictures of her mother and brothers. The miles between her two lives became a lesser obstacle. The beautiful home she returned to was not as lovely to her now. Her once stylish, pink bedroom no longer held the warmth and protection that it once did. The sheets were still stiff, and even surrounded by her books, she felt an unwelcome loneliness.

The household functioned much as it did before her trip. The most prominent change was the numerous post cards every week from Oklahoma with lots of responses from Vina. But things were not the same between Blanche and Vina. Blanche was always wanting to give her things, as if trying to make up for her lies, but Vina wasn't particularly receptive. Arthur was her only remaining anchor to this life. She loved it when he came home at the end of the day and announced his presence. As before, there was very little said about her trip to Oklahoma. Vina thought it was disinterest, but later she thought of it as Blanche's protection of her secrets and lies. She could no longer call them mother and father. She carried her real mother in her heart, and she had actually hugged her real father.

A few nights after her arrival, Arthur returned home late after Vina should have been sleeping. She was still awake and could easily hear through the wall and see through the partially open door. She had been told he had a fiery Irish temper, but he was always gentle with her, and she had never actually seen it. Upon his late entrance into the kitchen, it appeared he had been in a fight. His clothes were torn and his shirt bloody from a bleeding nose. She heard some sharp words from Blanche. The next morning, nothing was said, but Vina had the feeling this wasn't his first fight.

Shortly after her return, Vina's last year of school began. She'd shared stories of her trip with Fiona, who was always anxious to hear about anything adventurous. Her friend was totally enamored by the picture of Vina and her brothers. She picked out Bolivar for herself because she thought he was the most handsome. Vina didn't get it, since he was such a tease and annoyance to her as her brother. Vina learned that Blanche had told people that "Vina is visiting my family in Oklahoma." It angered her, but she saw no purpose in contradicting her. When she returned to school, everyone wanted to hear about her adventure, but no one else knew the purpose of her visit. Her classmates asked lots of questions: Did you see any Indians? Yes. Were they on the warpath? Thankfully, no. Was the dirt really red? Yes. And on and on....

At the end of the school year, Vina enjoyed the fun—a crazy dress up day and a frolic day with girlfriends. Blanche encouraged her to attend an end of school dance, promising her a shopping trip and a new dress. It just didn't seem worth the trouble to Vina, and she chose not to go; she found the boys at events like this were immature, unruly and annoying. The girls all talked about their futures, but Vina was unsure about what to do with her upcoming independence. She also felt resigned that she couldn't trust most people and needed to look out for herself. Blanche wanted her to attend a newly established school for higher learning near Vivian and live at home, but home did not feel much like home anymore. While her thirst for knowledge was great, Vina knew she needed to be on her own.

After graduation, many of her girlfriends started actively looking for suitors or headed in different directions. Vina went back to Oklahoma and the Knight family for the summer. She reconnected with her family and seemed to know herself better this visit. There was none of the awkwardness of trying to fit in. She returned to Vivian in late July, and with a couple of girlfriends moved to Leesville, Louisiana, only a hundred and fifty miles away, but far enough from Forest Street that she could live her own life without either of her families. Numerous people had told them that the town offered many jobs. Arthur said he had traveled to the town and was impressed by the rapid progress there. He saw thriving businesses and lots of opportunity.

With very little conversation and many warnings from Blanche, Vina packed her suitcase with her clothes and her mother's Bible, and left Vivian for good.

The Telephone Company, 1908

CHAPTER EIGHT

New Opportunities

In 1897, the Kansas City Southern Railway connected to Vernon Parrish. Heavy timber could finally be moved to larger markets, and Leesville started to grow. Ten years later, when Vina was looking for a place to move, it was perfect! The newspaper said it was thriving, and jobs, even for women, were being created daily. She could teach, work in a factory or in a household, or as a telephone operator.

Vina and her friends Fiona and Sallie arrived at the train station early on a Sunday morning, tickets in hand, ready for their trip. They waited on the platform, hoping to be the first to board. Vina saw that Arthur had secretly gone ahead because he was there waiting for them. When he said goodbye, he handed Vina a piece of paper with the address of a boarding house. He said that Miss Leona would be expecting them.

The young women arrived in the afternoon and made the short walk to downtown. The weather was unusually warm and lots of people milled around enjoying the sunshine. They headed straight to the address Arthur had given them. There on the front porch of a rather imposing three story building was Miss Leona. She was plump and pleasant and greeted them with hugs. She invited them inside to the parlor, offered them some tea, and began to tell them the rules of the boarding house. "No men allowed!

No liquor! No smoking! No loud noise! Clean up after yourself, and if you miss curfew, you will be sleeping on the street. Breakfast is served every morning at six and dinner is served every day but Sunday." She said that she would make us some sandwiches for dinner tonight. The friends looked at each other, wondering how many more rules she had.

They had chosen the third floor because it was cheaper and had a room for three. Carrying their luggage up the stairs, the girls got the giggles. They found their room before Miss Leona heard them. It was a small space, but larger than they'd expected, with three iron beds in a row along one wall, made up with colorful quilts. A dresser with a mirror, wash bowl and pitcher, and an armoire were on the opposite wall. There were also two small tables, each with a lamp in between the beds. It was probably not as nice as the bedrooms that they'd slept in the night before, but they thought it was absolutely lovely! The very best part of all was at the end of the hall—a bathroom! An inside bathroom, with a tub and a toilet and a sink with running water. Sallie's family had just put one in before she left, but neither Fiona nor Vina had inside plumbing yet.

After they settled in, the three went downstairs to the parlor and met a couple of the other roomers. They were very pleasant, but mostly talked about their boyfriends, a topic that held Sallie's interest. They played cards while other girls straggled in from afternoon outings. Vina and her friends were there for different reasons. Sallie was ok to work for a while since higher learning wasn't in her immediate future, and she hadn't found an acceptable mate in Vivian. She said that she needed to broaden her field of potential husbands. Fiona wanted to come because it was an adventure, and she says she hasn't ever been anywhere exciting. Vina needed to be away from her two families, be on her own and make her own money. She'd never really thought about money much before. Whatever she needed or occasionally wanted was always provided by Blanche and Arthur. Since she'd been home from her second trip to Oklahoma, she felt that Blanche's generosity and overzealous offers to buy things for her had become yet another effort to bend her will.

After they ate their sandwiches and checked out the bathroom, they went straight to bed. They talked a bit about their new experiences but went quickly to sleep. They hadn't signed up for the bathroom times, so when they awoke, they had a bit of a struggle to be ready for the day and downstairs by six am.

Newspaper articles suggested that working women, should wear only a long black skirt and a white high neck blouse. Their long hair should be piled up on their heads neatly. Depending on which job they choose, they might be able to have a bow at the neck. They read in the newspaper that the local telephone company was hiring that day starting at nine am. That seemed to be the job that all three were the most interested in, so they went out to explore the town right after breakfast. The town looked very different from yesterday. Lots of activity, people, carriages, delivery trucks, and horses. Today, being Monday, it seemed everyone was moving with a purpose. The three of them attracted a bit of attention from the residents, but the girls found it flattering.

As it approached their interview time, they made their way to the telephone company. About six women were already standing in line when they arrived. They bolstered each other's spirits and eavesdropped on conversations. Apparently, men had initially done this job, but most were terrible at it, handling irritated customers poorly and occasionally using vulgar language. Male employees couldn't follow rules or sit still without roughhousing, so the company had decided to replace them with women. It was thought that women would have better temperament for the job. The large doors opened, and the three friends were invited inside. Each was given a clip board and a pencil to fill out an application. The first line, as would be expected, was a place for the applicant's name. Vina had to pause a moment and think what to write. Oddly, she wasn't ready to deny either of her families. She quickly wrote Amanda Melvina Knight Pledger and hoped no one noticed her hesitation. She was then given a cursory interview and told to return at four o'clock.

They still didn't know very much about the job. In every part of town, workers had been busy putting up telephone poles and stringing wire. Vina and her friends returned to the company shortly before four o'clock and were invited inside. There were fifteen applicants, and all but two were offered a job. Those chosen accepted, none more rapidly than the three friends. They were told to return at seven o'clock the next morning for training and were expected to wear a black skirt and white blouse but no neck bows or jewelry. Elated at their quick success, they all wrote and mailed postcards home to share their good fortune.

Dinner at the boarding house was very animated. It reminded Vina of Oklahoma dinners with everyone talking at once. There were obvious cliques that had already been established, but the girls from Vivian talked among themselves, and the other women weren't unfriendly. One woman spoke of her bad experiences working as a telephone operator, but she didn't deter the friends. After dinner, they made sure they were ready to start their new jobs tomorrow. They went to bed early, but hardly slept with their new life just a few hours away.

The three tried to look sophisticated walking up the steps to the front door of The Telephone Company. They were greeted by a stern looking woman who then directed them to the employee entrance. Their training began at exactly seven am. Their manager was a man who explained the new technology and how all the wires worked to connect people together. To make a call, customers could not call others directly. The calls went to a central location and an intermediary would connect them. They would be that intermediary, a telephone operator. He took them into a windowless room with the equipment. They saw a bank of chairs in front of the board on a wall full of holes and cables and operators concentrating on their job. Later in the day they would be assigned to an operator who would show them how to do the job. Starting tomorrow, they would be on their own.

They returned to the training room, where they met their next instructor, a woman called Miss Belle. Sallie found that very amusing and was called out for snickering. From the start, Miss Belle established herself as strictly no nonsense. She was here to tell them the rules of their new job. They were to work nine to twelve-hour shifts with only one short break. They were to talk only to customers, never to each other, and no laughing. The strict dress code was no problem, but Fiona felt that no bows or jewelry was a bit much. They did some role playing about how to handle customers. Vina was surprised to find she was very good at role playing, and her confidence got the boost she needed. Miss Belle told them their wage amount, which they knew to be five cents an hour less than what the men they were replacing had been paid, but they were in no position to complain and were grateful for the opportunity.

The rest of the day was spent observing their mentors. It was a busy job, but not difficult; the pace made the day go quickly. The three reported the following day at the same time, but aware that they might be assigned to different shifts. They quickly adapted to their new jobs and schedules, and their first payday was a monumental day for the young friends. They paid Miss Leona, and what was left was fun money for Sallie and Fiona, but Vina considered it seed money for her future. Not that she didn't have fun; she just found much joy in the accumulation of cash.

The trio made the most of their newfound independence and their new town. Their days off were spent getting ready for the next week and also exploring the town. It was fun to live in a bustling community, where there was so much construction and progress. What amazing changes they saw, especially by the new ease of communication, and they felt a part of it. Vina enjoyed the pressure of handling five phone lines at once, each with multiple customers, and doing her job accurately. After a few weeks, Sallie had already turned the head of a proper suitor. None of the three mentioned being home sick.

Sallie had the most trouble sitting still. She was fine if they were busy, but instead of enjoying the slower times, she tried to make jokes or was subtly disruptive. Fortunately, her newly formed relationship with Alexander from New Orleans moved at a rapid pace. He was here working on a construction crew, and he just thought she was so cute and funny. They were married within the year and moved to Southern Louisiana, the perfect place for her.

Fiona had also met someone, but like Vina, she still enjoyed her job. She was taking her relationship slowly even though she slept on the front porch one night after missing curfew. Miss Leona did take her a blanket. Vina didn't go out much and preferred the books and games in the parlor. She was introduced to some eligible men but was always the one to break it off.

After a year and a half, Fiona was married, and Vina had moved into a nice single room, still on the third floor at Miss Leona's. Her cash stash was growing, and the many postcards back and forth kept her in touch with her families. But she felt no pull to return to Oklahoma or to Vivian. She received a postcard from Arthur that he would be in town on her day off and would like to spend some time with her. Vina looked forward to his arrival and even met him at the train station. He took her to a very nice restaurant in the newly built hotel. She told him all about her life, and he reported on happenings in Vivian. Blanche had been melancholy since Vina had left. There had been a change in the household, and his mother, Eugenia, from

Mississippi had moved in with them. Both women had strong personalities, and he worried how they would get along. So far, they seemed to enjoy each other's company, and Blanche even let his mother cook occasionally. He still traveled with work, so if it got tense at home, he said he just left and let them work it out. He admitted to gaining weight already.

Risdon was especially good about writing to Vina. The Knight family was rapidly expanding. He had a new baby girl, Emma Pauline, and another baby on the way. Jeff had a son, David, born less than a year after his daughter, Artie Melvina. Fortunately, Jeff became a full-time minister and was available to the family for christenings and other occasions. One of the memorable letters described the health of Vina's father. In his middle fifties, he had many health issues, most notably respiratory difficulties. He was not preaching or teaching any more but had become a peddler. He had joined a Masonic lodge. His youngest son, Alfred was a big help to him. Boliver, now called "Dock," had married, had a child, and moved away. No one had heard from him in quite a while. The news of this family was always welcome, but Vina still had no desire to visit.

She was very content with her life. Her job was busy, but dealing with customers, it was never boring. Vina pursued her love of reading again limiting herself to buying only one book a month and trading books with other boarders. After almost two years, she had been working there longer than most other operators and was no longer scrutinized by management. That worked to her advantage when one day she received a very intriguing telephone call.

1908 Telephone Operator

CHAPTER NINE

New Connection

Operator: "Number please."

Caller: "Is this Vina Knight Pledger?"

Operator: "Yes, sir. To what number may I connect you, sir"?"

Caller: "I already have the right number. I am O.V. Summers, and we were introduced by a friend yesterday. Are you available for dinner tonight at eight o'clock?"

Operator: "Yes, sir."

Caller: "I'll pick you up at eight then." The caller rang off.

And so it began.

Theirs was a courtship mostly by phone and kept secret even from the other operators. For the first time a man had held her interest. O.V. was a lineman and had been in The Telephone Building many times and noticed all the girls, but he was intensely attracted to the beautiful redhead. He felt like she was too proper to just call her without an introduction. Using his many contacts, he found out her name and where she lived, and he arranged a brief encounter with her so they could be properly introduced. His job of lineman, a new profession, was very well paid, but also dangerous as two out of three workers were killed in accidents. Training had made it safer, but most of the job, he had to learn on his own. O.V. was attracted to the electrical skills needed, the danger, and the money. He had an outgoing salesman's personality but took his job very seriously and was already a manager. In his newest position, he did have to travel some to troubleshoot problems. Hooking up his lineman's phone while on the top of a telephone pole was genius, risky, but genius, nevertheless.

Their first date was satisfying for both O.V. and Vina. They dined at the same hotel where she had gone with Arthur. O.V.'s manners were impeccable, he was very attentive, and encouraged conversation. He explained all of his efforts to make that call to her switchboard from a telephone pole, and she was flattered. Getting ready for bed that night, she was hoping to see him again.

Every time he returned from a business trip, he called her and tried to arrange to see her. At work on the call board, she would find herself hoping every caller on the other end of the line was him. She realized that it was totally absurd when she said "Number please" a hundred and twenty times an hour during her busiest times. Vina found O.V. charming, and he appeared to be quite successful for his age, only one year older than she. He was tall and trim with a warm smile, twinkling blue eyes, and a very pleasant clean-shaven face. She liked how manly he was, a man's man who always shook another man's hand while looking him in the eye. Always fun, but still proper, neatly dressed, with his hat at a jaunty angle. On some of their dates they played cards, sat on Miss Leona's front porch for hours, or visited some of the many new attractions in town. He also loved to show her off as they walked through town or went out to lunch or dinner. Her friends had all met him and had told her that if things didn't work out for them, please pass him on to the other girls.

Vina could tell from some of O.V.'s conversations that he was beginning to think about his future as their future. There had been a few stolen kisses and many hugs which she admitted that she had enjoyed.

She felt safe with him, probably safer than any time since her background had been revealed to her, and it was a long time before she trusted him enough to tell him her history. It became increasingly obvious to her that he wanted a traditional wife.

She did not want to lose him, but she knew that she could never be the subservient wife he imagined for himself. Vina gathered up her nerve to tell him before facing the embarrassment of declining a proposal. So, she brought up the subject at the end of another lovely evening. Fortified with a glass of wine at dinner, Vina began explaining the reasons she was going to end this relationship. "O.V., first of all, I love my job, and I would be required to quit if I married," she began. "I like making my own money and not having to explain to anyone how I spend it. I love to read and learn, and I want to further my education. I could not be the perfect wife you deserve." A last hug, some tears, and she went to her room expecting to never see him again.

That night O.V. reflected on all the things he loved, yes, loved about Vina. He had never spoken that word out loud except to his family. He was initially attracted to her beauty, her luscious red hair which he imagined falling to her shoulders, her slate blue eyes, her incredibly beautiful skin and smile. He adored her posture and the confidence she showed in her step. Although he felt totally at ease with her, he always had to remain sharp to meet her mind. She graciously accepted his compliments but never took his words all that seriously. Many times before, the effect of his well-placed compliments had softened a girl's will, but those charms didn't work on Vina, which he found rather amusing. He had never met a woman so strong, and he had to dramatically change his approach. That night she had completely shut him down. "I believe in my future," he thought to himself, "Who wouldn't want to share it on my terms.? Vina, that's who!" He considered the dilemma for a couple of days. At work, he was so preoccupied with those thoughts that while connecting a line, he almost made a mistake that could have cost him his life.

Vina also was reflecting on her past and her path forward. She immediately realized she was better at knowing what she didn't want than what she did want. She was happy with her life. Her job wasn't as much fun now but was serving her purpose. One of the operators that had been there for a year longer had been promoted to a supervisor and had received a decent raise which made Vina feel like she could have a future with this company.

Thinking about the wives in both of her families, and the roles they played, she realized that those lifestyles wouldn't work for her. She found no comfort in reviewing them both. The Oklahoma wives birthed children, almost one after another. They were subservient to their husbands. They had no time or interest for anything but children and home. None had furthered their education, and a few were leading lives of drudgery. They seemed to love their husbands but were mostly bored by them, all while being mostly dependent on their spouse for survival.

Blanche, on the other hand, was not subservient and ruled her "roost." Vina adored Arthur, but aside from the loving relationship that she had with him, she felt he was a coward around Blanche. She certainly didn't want a husband who couldn't stand up to her.

Vina came to the conclusion that it was the right thing to break off her relationship with O.V. Maybe she loved him, maybe she was just infatuated, but she simply could not live the traditional role of a wife, certainly not now. She didn't see herself as a spinster and thought she might like a child or two someday, but never six or eleven. She felt her decision was best for them both. It would free up O.V. to have the traditional home and family he wanted, and she would be just fine on her own for a while longer.

O.V. 1909

Vina, 1909

CHAPTER TEN

Amanda Melvina Knight

Vina awoke to a deliciously miserable morning which exactly matched her mood. It had rained all night, and the air in her room was stifling. She arose from her bed feeling none of her usual enthusiasm for a new day. She wasn't ill, maybe a little bit sad. She had trouble fixing her hair. It behaved like it really would rather be worn down all day, but that certainly couldn't happen. She dressed, ate breakfast quickly, and headed out the door. She needed her umbrella, even though it was only a short walk to work. She normally looked forward to the walk, regardless of the weather, but today it seemed like a monumental task. Avoiding puddles and good morning pleasantries, she made it to work. When she walked into the building, she straightened her back, went to her chair and right to work.

"Number, please."

Vina rarely allowed her mind to wander at work because she was busy every minute of her shift, but thoughts crept into her mind all day. It had been five days since she'd said goodbye to O.V. "I don't want to marry anyone," she thought to herself, "but I admit to missing his company." She'd heard today that he has been out of town, so she decided maybe that's why he hadn't contacted her. Another day passed, and she fell deeper into an unwelcome melancholy.

The very next day on her way home from work, however, she felt a familiar pep in her step and was looking forward to the evening. She rounded the corner, and there on the front porch was O.V. looking even more dapper than usual, with a big smile on his face.

"Good evening, Miss Pledger. Would you consider taking a walk with me to a new café in town?" Of course she agreed, as she was anxious to spend time with him. He made casual conversation, and she invented activities to tell him about. He was full of news. He had been out of town in Beaumont, Texas. Vina had read that Beaumont was booming due to oil and timber with a population of over 20,000 and still growing. O.V. told her he'd taken a new job with a major company, The Texas Company in Beaumont. "They need my electrical expertise, and I will be well paid with lots of opportunity for advancement," he told her.

Vina could feel his enthusiasm, and it sounded like an exciting place to live and work. She was happy for him, but Beaumont was a long way away from here. They toasted his new adventure and enjoyed a very nice dinner until the restaurant had emptied. It was totally quiet!

And then O.V. spoke, breaking the silence in the virtually empty room. "Vina, I want...no, I need you to come with me to Beaumont as my wife. Before you answer, I have given a great deal of thought about your reasons not to be married. First, you'll quit your job because you are moving, not because you are getting married. I really would prefer that my wife not work outside our home; however, I am aware that you want your own money. Would you consider a generous allowance or consider pay for managing our household. I promise to never ask what you spend the money on. There will be plenty of other money for you to furnish our home. I would like to have children, but only when you are ready, and only how many you wish. In a large city like Beaumont, there are many opportunities for you to learn, and many women's groups you can join.

I can provide you the life you want by compromising, and I promise to honor and cherish you always...." He paused, and she saw him swallow hard, then he took in a deep breath and said, "So what do you think?"

Vina was startled, and her heart raced. She said, "That's a great deal to think about, and I'll need a little time." O.V. told her he had only ten days before he started his new job. They walked back to Miss Leona's arm in arm, and Vina's mind was racing as fast as her heart. They kissed a very long kiss and hug that she didn't want to end, but after lingering a bit, they said goodnight.

In her room, her thoughts seemed to collide with a million questions: that was a great deal of sweet talk, she thought, and it touched her deeply, but how could she know he was sincere? What if they got to Beaumont, and he felt like he won the prize, and a beautiful house becomes her prison with him as her guard? How could she keep her independence and still be a wife? The money does make a difference, and if she was to be honest with herself, there really wasn't that much opportunity for women at The Telephone Company, or at any other job for that matter. This was a world totally dominated by men, and women were left out of everything. Here it is already the twentieth century, and we can't even vote, she mused, and on legal documents, we are sometimes told to sign 'Wife,' not even our proper names. Men still needed women to make babies, but Vina had read that there where new methods to help women decide when they want to have a child.

What O.V. offered her was a huge compromise on his part. He could maintain his male society persona, but in their home, they would share more than just a bed, assuming that he didn't go back on his word. Vina didn't expect an equal marriage. That is preposterous, never in a million years would that happen! She knew he was a flirt and appreciated women for their charm, but something deep inside told her that his commitment to her was real, and that he expected, as she did, that it was forever. Vina lay awake all night pondering his offer. She hated that there was a deadline involved, so she looked to another source for help. Her mother's Bible had been in her room for the more than two years that she'd lived there. She occasionally opened it and read scriptures, but this time she needed God and the strength of her mother to help make her decision. She could almost hear her mother saying, "Vina, this is the life I dreamed of for you." Vina could scarcely imagine the short life her mother had as it would compare to hers.

She read parts of the Bible that she hadn't read before, starting with Genesis 2:18-24.

> *"And the Lord God said, It is not good for the man to be alone: I will make him a helper suitable for him. ......and the rib that the Lord God had taken from the man he made into a woman and brought her to the man. And the man said: This is now bone of my bones and flesh of my flesh; she shall be called Woman, because she was taken out of Man. Therefore man shall leave his father and his mother and hold fast to his wife, and they shall become one flesh."*

And then, God, her mother, and Vina decided it was time for her to be a wife.

After that, she felt totally at ease with her decision. She was anxious to tell O.V. but had to wait until after work tomorrow. She considered asking him to write his promises down but chose instead to have faith in God, him, and their future. Besides, she'd memorized every word he'd said, just in case she might need to bring it up.

CHAPTER ELEVEN

Amanda Melvina Knight Summers

O.V. was waiting outside the employee entrance when Vina finished work the next day. He wanted to know immediately if she had decided on his proposal. She had, but wanted just a bit more privacy to answer, and so they went back to Miss Leona's front porch. O.V. was ecstatic with her yes! He picked her up and spun her around while yelling "she said yes!" He made such a scene that Miss Leona invited him into the parlor, or "no man's land" as the girls called it. Producing a beautiful diamond ring from his pocket, he got down on one knee and put the ring on her finger. The few girls who were around thought it was the most romantic thing they had ever seen and were actually swooning over the scene before them. Miss Leona, much to everyone's surprise, brought out a hidden bottle of wine for a toast. So far, they had broken at least three rules that were thought to be cast in stone. Here is to many more broken rules! Vina toasted.

Suddenly overwhelmed, Vina wondered how she could ever complete her tasks ahead—to quit her job, figure out a wedding, make a 250 mile move, and set up a new home with a new husband, and be in control of the outcomes. She thanked God that she didn't have to move in a covered wagon like her mother.

O.V. was so cocky, she was somewhat surprised that he hadn't already rented a house for them. Maybe he wasn't sure of her answer after all. Doubt about anything was a rare side to him, but Vina found that charming. Quitting her job was not as difficult as she expected. The turnover rate was high, and she didn't even have to wait for a replacement. After quitting, she saw her job from a different perspective. Yes, it allowed her some independence, but the pay was low and certainly less than the men's. The girls were so controlled, indentured almost, even to their personal lives by not allowing married women to continue working. All of the supervisors and managers except one were men. Life was changing for Vina, but she would never forget the good and bad of the job or the plight of her coworkers.

The opportunity arose to talk to Arthur about her decision to drop his name, Pledger. To her knowledge no official paperwork had ever been filed. Being his usual self, he was supportive and said he understood. From then on, she was to be known as Amanda Melvina Knight Summers, enough names for anyone.

Miss Leona enthusiastically offered to plan their wedding at the boarding house, and the bride easily accepted her offer. They invited both families, actually all three families, to join them, but on such short notice, very few came. Arthur was definitely coming, but Blanche felt she needed to stay with Eugenia who was ill. Vina's father wasn't up to the trip either, but Risdon and Jeff came to meet this man who was taking their sister away. The day her brothers arrived, they took O.V. out for the evening, and for the next two days they were together smoking cigars, drinking and getting acquainted. All three men had Vina's best interests at heart, and they reached the understanding that Vina and O.V. would make a trip to Oklahoma soon for him to meet the rest of her family, and they could meet her new husband. On the second day, the rowdy group was joined by

Arthur, and vows were made by each one to always protect Vina!

It was mid September, and the weather was delightful. Vina chose a simple white linen dress with lace trim. She wore her hair up as was proper, but with a hat that Miss Leona said she needed to complete her outfit. Both the wedding and reception were outside in a side yard at the boarding house. Choosing from among Risdon, Jeff, or Arthur to walk her up the aisle invited more drama than she cared to create, so Vina walked the aisle by herself, toward her handsome groom, full of joy and ready for commitment.

Several of her operator friends and a few girls from the boarding house and friends of O.V. came, which made for the perfect gathering. Miss Leona seemed very friendly with Arthur and was sad when he left. When Vina moved to Leesville, Arthur had recommended the boarding house to her, and she recalled he'd been very enthusiastic about Miss Leona. She wondered briefly if there was more than friendship between them.

After spending two nights in the hotel, the newlyweds gathered her few belongings and said their goodbyes, and they were off to their new life as Mr. and Mrs. Summers.

OV & Arthur Toasting the Bride, 1910

PART THREE

CHAPTER TWELVE

The Newlyweds

Much to Vina's surprise, there were several people at the train station to see them off to Beaumont. Miss Leona brought them a food basket. Arthur, who hadn't yet left town, came with a few friends and brought her a lovely bouquet of flowers. As O.V. helped his bride up the stairs of their train, she felt pure joy, secure in herself, her husband, and her future. The trip took eight hours with many stops, but they had a wonderful time laughing, hugging, and planning. O.V. was such a good storyteller that he could entertain her for hours.

On their nighttime arrival, Vina was surprised at how lit up the town was with electric lights. O.V. had spent a great deal of time here working and explained that it was a priority of the city. He also led her to believe, laughingly, that he was responsible for every single light. A buggy took them to a hotel, and the next day they awoke in their new town. O.V. had arranged for them to see three houses for rent that could be occupied immediately. It was totally Vina's choice, he repeated, and he even stayed outside while she explored the possibilities. She chose the mid-sized one with the large front porch. They all had indoor bathrooms, thank God.

That afternoon they shopped for a bed and table with two chairs. Using his charm, O.V. made a deal with the owner for them to be delivered the next day. The following morning, they moved into their new home with their very few possessions, mainly a few household items and sheets that were gifts from the wedding. On the mantle over the fireplace Vina discovered two envelopes, one marked "Household" and the other, "Vina's Money." Both contained very generous amounts. This reoccurred monthly for many years until they became deposits into her two bank accounts. The marriage so far, after four days, was off to a good start.

This was a Friday, and Monday, O.V. would be off to work so they so they dined out for the first three nights because Vina hadn't yet developed any cooking skills. Saturday, the stores were open, and O.V. helped her learn how to ride the street cars to get where she needed to shop. Sunday, Vina suggested that they go to see the newly renovated church in town, St. Anthony. Neither of them was Catholic, but she wanted to see the inside of the church and its world-renowned stained glass windows. They were in total awe as they walked inside. Neither had seen such beauty, nor had they been inside a church together. They held hands, kneeled when others knelt, but refrained from going to the altar. O.V. didn't care for the service but seemed to enjoy sharing the experience with his wife. Except for asking God to help her make the decision to get married, she hadn't thought about HIS role in their marriage. They had discussed their faith before, but not in terms of their marriage. Vina sensed that that would be better left for another day.

O.V. was always very loving and patient with her, but sooner or later, the man needed to eat. After a meager breakfast on Monday, he was out the door, and Vina decided to make a real effort to learn to cook for her husband. Blanche was a wonderful cook, and Vina wished she'd paid more attention when she lived with her, instead of always reading or doing something else. Blanche didn't seem to relish anyone in her kitchen anyway. Vina wrote her a postcard asking for recipes, but she needed more immediate help. She went to the nearby grocery store and muddled through the first few meals.

Vina was surprised at how much she enjoyed her new role as a wife, and she loved being in her own home. Remnants of a vegetable garden were evident in the small yard, and another garden by the steps looked like flowers had grown there before. She had seen some seeds at a store, so she decided to try to grow flowers in the yard.

Vina relished the one major indulgence in her first home, an inviting claw foot tub with a shower. She liked nothing more than a long soaking bath with warm water and the opportunity to properly wash her hair, in the middle of the day if she chose, with the window open if the weather allowed, and a hint of lavender oil in the bath. She sometimes just let her hair hang to well below her shoulders to dry, brushing it occasionally.

O.V. came home early one day when she still had her hair down and was barefoot and wearing just a loose fitting dress. He opened the door, always in a rush, took off his hat, then stopped and stared at her. She stammered an apology for her appearance, but he cut her short. "Vina, you are the most beautiful woman I have ever seen. Your eyes, your skin, your hair, your smile. I am truly blessed that you are my wife." Vina was deeply touched when she saw a tear in his eye when he kissed her. Dinner was late and not particularly good, but neither cared. From that day on, if she knew she would not be going out, she often wore her hair down or tied back with a ribbon. Not the style of the day, but she loved the freedom, and her husband loved to run his fingers through her soft wavy hair.

Vina made friends with her next-door neighbor, a very nice woman named Annie who was just a few years older than she and from Oklahoma. Annie helped her with shopping, cooking, and things like how to handle getting milk and ice delivered. Annie was a talented cook and after learning the basics, Vina was surprised at how much she enjoyed the process. Fortunately, O.V.'s tastes were fairly simple. Vina also received a long letter from Blanche with recipes and household tips. It was good to hear from her, and the new homemaker welcomed her advice. Blanche had been her mother for a long time, and she had kept an immaculate home. One of her suggestions to the new bride was to use milk to shine her wood floor. A vision of her mother's dirt floors crept into her thoughts as she read the letter; what must that have been like? Vina paused and said a little prayer for her mother, something she did often.

Blanche's decorating had always seemed very stylish, and Vina enjoyed growing up around beautiful things. She never considered herself spoiled, but after meeting her Oklahoma relatives, and living in different places, she realized that she did live a very comfortable lifestyle compared to many. Fortunately, her husband was motivated to continue to provide for that. The difficult part for her would be not to lose herself in the process.

In the evenings, they often sat on their large front porch if weather allowed and visited with passersby, or just enjoyed each other's company. Cigars had become a part of O.V.'s style and he agreed to smoke them only outside. Vina didn't really mind the smell but disliked the ashes. Inside, they often read and talked in front of the fireplace. O.V. read mostly technical journals and the newspaper, and Vina still read books and poetry, often reading her favorite poems out loud to O.V. Recently, she had been introduced to women's magazines. After subscribing to Good Housekeeping and McCall's, she was still amazed that they actually came in the mail weekly, and she devoured the modern living information. The magazines held abundant stories of housekeeping hints, recipes, patterns for sewing, and even occasionally world news.

There was also a great deal of advice, much of which were tips on how best to talk to your husband. She was attracted to a questionnaire with questions for a husband and wife to ask each other to promote conversation and approached O.V. on a quiet evening at home. They didn't get through even two questions about the husband's feelings before he made it very obvious that he wasn't answering any "cream puff" questions. She often wondered where he got that word and thought about the evening, laughing to herself that she'd even tried it.

Christmas was just a couple of weeks away. The husband surprised his wife by bringing a small Christmas tree home, complete with a string of bubble lights. She had never seen anything like them. They were probably the only people in the neighborhood with electric lights on a tree. They decorated it with ribbons, berries and popcorn. Vina began the tradition of buying a couple of delicate glass Christmas ornaments for her tree and added to her collection every year. It was the most beautiful tree either one had ever seen!

O.V. surprised his wife by telling her that he made delicious eggnog, and he wanted to have a party, to invite neighbors and friends over on Christmas Day to share some eggnog. Vina panicked. In spite of having very little time and very few places to sit, Vina rose to the occasion as always. She relied on tips from her magazines and Blanche, and they had the first of many Christmas Day open houses.

O.V.'s eggnog was stout, but he also had a children's bowl in which she dipped her cup. When they reflected on the day, they were both very pleased at their joint entertaining. He was a warm inviting host, and even though Vina had always considered herself to be shy, when she had a house full of people and there was no place to hide, she mingled, served people, and had an unexpectedly delightful time. Their house was ample, but it didn't take many people to fill it up, and the event brought them both much pleasure and was a prelude to their future social life.

Vina's Christmas gift from O.V. was the sewing machine that she had asked for, but having no skills, learning to sew was her new project. After Christmas, he began to travel as part of his job. It was only for a few days at a time, and she enjoyed being able to work on projects without having to stop to cook dinner. His homecomings were always wonderful.

By the middle of January, Vina was not feeling as perky as usual and occasionally even took a nap. She feared she was getting lazy since she wasn't working. Soon, the reason for her changes in routine became obvious to her. She felt life in her belly. Telling O.V. that he was going to be a father was one of the most precious moments of their lives. Knowing that he wanted a family, and he was always a bit impatient, she knew he would be thrilled that it would happen sooner than later. She was happy too, but also terrified. He dropped a couple of hints...that he would really like a son...which didn't help her at all. How could she guarantee that? She'd never been around newborns and had seen her nieces and nephews only a few times. Once again, calling on her faith, she was sure that with God's help, she could handle it.

Her pregnancy was an idyllic time for her. She had very little queasiness and soon regained her energy. The months went by quickly, and she used the time to work on decorating her house. Blanche had always said, "When you buy a piece of furniture, wait until you can afford what you really want. If you compromise, you will be stuck with it forever." Vina took her advice to heart and took her time making decisions. One of her first purchases was a walnut chest with a marble top. When it was delivered, she was in a quandary of where to place it. The house was so empty of furniture that she could have used four of them. But she made careful choices, and one chest was enough for now. Her neighbor, Annie, taught her how to use her sewing machine and make curtains. Vina still wrote lots of postcards, but now with real news to impart to their families.

As her bulk increased, Vina was ready to deliver this baby. She gave birth with help of a midwife to a handsome baby boy on August 6, 1911, Frederic Gordon Summers. The new father was ecstatic! It was a Sunday, and he didn't need to call anyone because he yelled the news from the front porch and passed out cigars.

The following year, the beloved postcards brought the devastating news that Risdon had died. A letter followed written by their brother, Jeff, explaining that Risdon had respiratory problems and was ill several weeks prior to his death. Vina wrote back with condolences that seemed to her to be very inadequate. His death was life changing to her: she no longer had her savior, her protector, her lifeline to her mother. She felt sorry for his wife, Emma, and his children, especially Maud who was now fourteen years old and almost a woman. Vina was deeply concerned about how his family would survive, but she knew that Jeff and James were nearby and hoped they would take care those left behind. No one had seen or heard from Bolivar for a couple of years when word came that he had also died and left a widow and child.

O.V. offered to arrange a trip for her to go to Oklahoma for a visit, if she felt the need to go; however with a very young child a trip would be impractical, and she doubted that she could be of any help, especially with a baby in tow. She grieved alone for her brother but was grateful for the part that he had played in her life, and he would remain in her heart forever. Vina had never told the story of her early childhood to anyone else, ever.

Vina, out with a friend, 1912

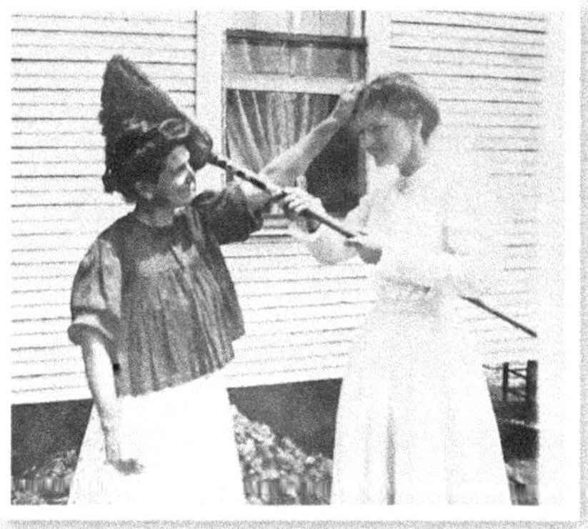

New Brides' fun with a friend, 1910

Shreveport, Louisiana 1912

CHAPTER THIRTEEN

Back Home to Shreveport

Settling into their new life as a family was not as smooth as she had hoped. Busy with the added care of a child and keeping house, Vina considered that Frederic could be an only child, even though her body had recovered quickly, and surprisingly childbirth was not at all as horrendous as she had been told. Her instincts took over where her knowledge was lacking, and the three of them had to adjust to the changes in their routines. Blanche offered to come and help her, but with this birth, Vina felt much closer to her deceased mother, Melviney, than to Blanche, so she declined.

When she held their child, Vina was amazed at the love, more love than she thought she was capable of, as it poured out of every measure of her being. Even though she'd listened carefully to her father and brothers' description of Melviney's caring and love for her, she did not truly understand that love until she experienced for herself. She wept at the overwhelming connection she felt to her mother, instantly understanding the dreams Melviney had held for all of her children. Vina thanked God for her life and her healthy child and prayed that she would be worthy to rear this child in HIS name.

After four months, the Summers' household was thriving. O.V. was all about Frederic! From the moment the new father flew into the house, he wanted to hold his son, even if his mother had just put him down for a nap. Frederic was a happy healthy baby and, most importantly, very adaptable to the quiet during the day and louder playtime of the evening. On a Tuesday, O.V. came home with his usual big smile, called out for his son, and announced that the family was moving to Shreveport. Once again, a promotion for O.V. and a better life for his family would require another move. Vina was happy where they were, but O.V.'s ambition would always be the driving force of their lives.

Someone from O.V.'s company came to help her pack, so this move was easier for the lady of the house. Jourdan Street in Shreveport, Louisiana was their new address. The spaciousness of this home and the large wraparound porch made missing her previous neighbors and friends more tolerable. After two years of marriage, they had accumulated the necessary household items and a few special pieces of furniture. Still, the huge house seemed empty even with all their belongings, but she was undaunted. She would make it a home for her family!

She happily embraced the opportunity to rediscover Shreveport, a city that had always been special to her. Shopping with her very young companion and searching for furniture and accessories was a challenge. Frederic had his father's outgoing personality and always attracted attention which slowed down the outings. O.V. bought a new car and after many requests from his wife, he taught her to drive it. A woman behind the wheel of a car was not a common sight.

O.V. and Vina had discussed traveling with the new baby. O.V. wanted to take him to see his family in Jefferson, and Vina was missing her family and friends in Vivian. At O.V.'s encouragement, Frederic and his mother traveled to Vivian for a short visit. Although Frederic was an easy traveler, she was still apprehensive about the trip and finally seeing Blanche again. Arthur picked them up by buggy, and they went directly to her childhood home. While the house was certainly familiar, she no longer held all the conflicted feelings that she'd taken with her when she left. Blanche seemed happy to give her solicited advice about running her home. Arthur's mother, Eugenia, was now living there, and all three were delighted with Frederic. He had recently had his first birthday and was a fun, cheerful little boy.

They had some outbuildings on their property, a chicken coop, smokehouse, and a barn, as well as an aging farm horse, Old Blue. As young as he was, it was all a wonderful adventure for her son, and Arthur loved having another "farm hand." Somehow, time and motherhood had absorbed many of her past mixed emotions. Vina wanted Frederic to have the consistency of grandparents even if they weren't really related. By the time they left, Blanche and Arthur were called Mawmaw and Pawpaw, and she promised to return.

O.V. and Vina agreed that it was time to expand their family, and thankfully she had another healthy pregnancy. Their daughter, Ruth Louise Summers, was born at home, October 29, 1914. A family friend who was also a doctor delivered this perfect child. Of course, her father was beyond thrilled, refrained from yelling the news as before, but continued the cigar tradition. Vina felt as though she had done her job. One of each.

Settling into a family life of four was quite easy. Frederic adored Ruth and soon became known as Bubba. He pushed her in her pram, and as she grew, he loved having a playmate, especially on visits to Mawmaw and Pawpaw on their small farm. O.V. was still traveling but only for a few days at a time and the rest of the family adapted easily to his comings and goings. His responsibilities grew with his job, and he taught himself what he needed to learn to qualify for Professional Electric Engineer accreditation.

It was a happy time for them, and she relished being back in Louisiana. A highlight for Vina was the library in town, where she went as a child and loved the smells, the quiet and the mystery of the building as she meandered through the aisles stacked with books wanting to read every one. As an adult, she took her two children weekly and was delighted when her children also discovered a love of books. The building and the atmosphere inside brought her warm memories of the innocent part of her childhood and was always a place of peace and comfort to her.

They were living in one of the most volatile years to date in American history, 1919. Even though the War was officially over, extraordinary challenges loomed. Anarchist bombings, racial violence, labor unrest, and a return of an influenza epidemic. She read the "Shreveport Times" daily, and while her family had felt only a trickle of the problems reported, it started to seem to her that the parish officials were not being completely truthful about the influenza epidemic and the local quarantines that were established.

Commissioners ordered all schools, amusement centers, theaters, movie houses and churches be closed. Shreveport became a ghost town. She read that in her parish, more than one hundred people were dying a month. Younger children were at greatest risk. Homes with flu patients were asked to hang yellow placards in their front windows. More people died from influenza than in the Great War that had just ended. Vina was terrified. Citizens wore masks and had little contact with others during the isolation, which was wearing on their community. She became creative, cooking with the bounty from her garden, discovering new entertainment for her children, and leading an isolated but fulfilling life. O.V. had to continue to work, but with no added travel, they gratefully made it through the ordeal.

During this time, Vina made a statement of her own. Her husband loved her long auburn hair and said the color was what first attracted him to her. After hearing Risdon's stories of searching for her, she also felt it had been the transcendent reason that he had found her. However, the style of the day was to "bob" one's hair. O.V. was out of town once again, and she enjoyed reading a magazine after a long day juggling children and chores. She came across a compelling article, "To Bob or Not to Bob." She didn't immediately grab for the scissors, but she sat for a while in front of the mirror, holding her hair back and imagining it short. For the next couple of days, it remained in the back of her mind. After all, taking care of short hair must take less time, and she would be following the style of the day. For one of the few times in her married life, her decision wasn't based on what her husband would think. She already knew he wouldn't be pleased. She considered it to be a not-so-subtle reinforcement of her independence. In a meaningful act, not a spiteful one, she cut her hair! O.V. took it as a personal affront, but after seeing more and more women with short hair, and he always looked at women, he mentioned that perhaps she was a style setter. She wore her hair short the rest of her life.

As much as O.V. and Vina discussed the children, their lives, and the world, the conversation rarely touched on politics or social mores. For all his many compromises, he still had some irrevocable beliefs pertaining to women, which included his wife. She was very tuned in to the roles of working women and empathized with their struggles. She was well aware of birth control clinics being established in New York and was particularly interested in the Five Mile Suffrage Parade along Fifth Avenue, which occurred shortly after Ruthie was born. While she was not the demonstrating type, and O.V. would be aghast, she was in tune to those events and wholeheartedly supported women's rights.

The suffrage movement happened in the midst of the beginnings of World War I, and Vina continued to tiptoe around the subject. She found more power with her husband using subtle comments and asking him penetrating questions than overt conflict with him over issues of the day. This was the conservative South, and O.V. was a traditional white male of that time. His prejudices were taught and inherited as a part of his upbringing. Woven into his fiber were beliefs that could not be easily challenged or adjusted. She doubted that it was her role to instigate the conflict it would cause if she tried. Vina considered her role to be one of a more equal partner, and while some of his compromises seem small, they were huge to him, even including "allowing" her to drive her own car. Big changes take time, and she vowed to endeavor to make a better life for her son and daughters.

In Massachusetts, a mere ten years after she left her job at The Telephone Company, telephone operators, still mostly women, walked off their jobs. They took off their headsets and brought New England business to a standstill. Government officials and industry executives were totally caught off guard by the women's organization and determination. In less than a week, the company acquiesced to higher wages and better working conditions. Vina was thrilled and would have passed out cigars herself if she could, but the strike was never discussed in their household.

Christmas was quiet and without an eggnog party, but the children were joyful, and they had so much for which to be grateful. The beginning of 1920 brought normality back to lives. The library was back open, and the city came back to life quickly. She loved her home, even after being confined to it for over a year. She quickly returned to their comfortable lifestyle. The spaciousness of their home gave room for their family, even the newest one that was starting to move around in her belly.

During the summer, Vina made another trip to Vivian when Bubba and Ruthie were eight and five years old. They loved going to Pawpaw's farm. Vina enjoyed this trip more than any other because Blanche and Arthur had recently remodeled part of their porch to add an indoor bathroom. Being pregnant, Vina was definitely not looking forward to roughing it by the day's standards. Reflecting on how quickly humans adapt to new creature comforts made her think again about her mother's way of life. She enjoyed a break from cooking and was spoiled by the ladies of the house. When the travelers returned home, O.V. picked them up at the train station in a nice new touring car.

In 1920, when women were granted the franchise to vote, no one was happier than O.V. Summers, who gleefully announced that now he had two votes, his and that of his wife, Vina. Was he ever wrong! Not only did she refuse to promise to vote according to his mandate, but she also refused to tell him how she voted, ever!

The fall was one of her favorite times of the year. The children were flourishing. Bubba was not particularly enthusiastic about school, but happy to come home to Ruthie and play with the neighborhood kids. As time came closer to her delivery, she was actively trying to prepare their home and family for the new member. She was relieved that she finally had their lives stable. But about a week later, O.V. came home with news that he had received another big promotion in the corporate office in Houston. Prominence and fortune awaited him and his family, but it took a few days for her to absorb that they were going to move yet again. O.V. was so excited about his new job that she was, of course, happy for him. Luckily, her marriage had taught her a lot of things, most importantly, flexibility.

CHAPTER FOURTEEN

Move to Houston

O.V. assured Vina that this would be their last move. He would now be in the Main Office and head of a department, and even more promotions wouldn't take him out of the city. He made a trip to Houston without his very pregnant wife to find a home. This time he would purchase their home, but there weren't many from which to choose. As he visited the area, there were only two sections of the city within his budget that interested him. He arrived during heavy spring rains and discovered that only the Houston Heights and the East End were high and dry, and that the rest of the small city was drowning in flood waters. There were only a few new homes being built, and he purchased a locked one without inspecting the inside. He chose it from standing outside in the mud and looking in through the windows at 447 West 16th Street in a very modest Heights' neighborhood. The house was minimum in size

Vina & Mawmaw, 1920

with only two bedrooms and one bathroom, not nearly adequate for his growing family, but it was the largest available lot and he had plans.

Vina was less than pleased when he recounted his purchase. Since there were no other options, and she had resolved not have this baby before they moved, she quickly started packing up their belongings once again and passed another test of her continuing flexibility.

The Summers' house became the nicest house in the neighborhood. O.V. lost no time in improving the property, planting trees, installing landscaping, adding another bedroom, and a large screened-in back porch as a second living/dining room. There was a one car garage with another building in the backyard called "the woodhouse," where stove wood was stored. Also in that building there was equipment for laundry: a bench for tubs, water faucets, and scrub wash boards. Laundry was intensive hand labor, with heavy wet laundry hung with peg clothes pins on lines in the backyard. On the other hand, milk, ice and fresh produce were delivered to their door, and a grocery store was only a block away.

Vina ran her home with the help of Lena, a Negro laundress/maid who sometimes brought one of her children with her. Vina's children were allowed to play with hers but had to stay out of sight in the back yard. It was the mores of the day. Vina was taught and taught her children, not so much by her words but her actions, that Negros were inferior to whites. One day Ruthie came running inside after playing with one of Lena's children. He had scraped his knee, and it bled. Ruthie was delighted to report the discovery to her mother then and later to the family at dinner, that the Negro boy's blood looked just like hers! Her father's abrupt response ended the conversation.

Shortly after the Summers family moved into their completely unsatisfactory house, Vina gave birth on November 4, 1920, to her second little girl, Rosemary Vina Summers. She was a beautiful, round-faced pink baby with a scattering of dark hair and was quickly called "Baby" by the whole family. The cigars came out again, and O.V. loved to boast that he now had a redhead, a blond and a brunette!

O.V. received a company car so his wife always had a family car available to her. Houston, itself was starting to show signs of the great city it would become. The paved roads were splendid, but when it rained, it was impossible to drive through the muddy unpaved ones. She had heard that Houston was referred to as the "Bayou City" but didn't know that she would often have to deal with water occasionally overflowing the banks of White Oak Bayou. O.V. had become a Mason and was also getting more socially active with his work friends, while Vina's sphere included church attendance, Sunday School, meetings of the Missionary Society and other organizations. Christian Endeavor for the children, Deacons' meetings for O.V., as well as church socials at Heights Presbyterian were prominent in their lives.

More houses were built to add to the substantial brick homes along the well-known Heights Blvd, although most of the homes in their area were still wooden Victorian style. But more houses and more paved roads brought more families with neighborhood kids of varying backgrounds. Vina became concerned that the neighborhood girls were receiving no training in social skills, so she organized a group including Ruth, (Rosemary was too young,) with the goal of trying to make them into ladies. She named the group, "Little Women" and with a few prayers gave it her best shot. The enthusiastic group met at her home regularly and had lessons on being a good hostess, how to greet and treat guests, how to serve gracefully and set a proper table, and how to make one's way through a meal of several courses knowing which utensils to use. She included proper dress for different occasions and importantly, how to make a graceful exit from a function. She hoped that her daughters would learn by her example but doubted that any of the other girls would have another opportunity to learn social graces. Vina often told Ruth and Rosemary individually, "I'll make a lady out of you if it kills us both."

O.V. always liked to be the center of attention and never more so than the day he showed the family a primitive crystal radio that he had made. Radio broadcasts were in their infancy. The main problem was that his radio had headphones, and only one person at a time could hear. So, he rigged a loudspeaker, which consisted of the radio placed on a towel inside a galvanized bucket resting on its side. The sound quality was terrible, but the whole family could all hear. This set-up was soon followed by a more sophisticated radio set in a cabinet. Radio receivers for the home market developed rapidly, but the Summers were the first in their neighborhood to own one.

O.V. loved games, board games, card games, games of any kind, and was an expert at all of them. He insisted that the children become bridge players, and he oversaw their progress. He organized croquet games in his large back yard. It was a man's game and fought like war. The fenced court was a raked sand field like a Japanese garden, and children were not allowed inside the fence. He built a playhouse for Rosemary, with many of the amenities of a full-size house. He also built a chicken yard and coop to raise his prize Plymouth Rocks. His big white rooster, proudly named "Texaco," awakened the neighborhood each morning with his stentorian crow.

A memorable New Year's morning in 1924 brought an unusual phenomenon into their Heights home. While playing cards with the children, Vina's whole body shuddered. The children were wide eyed with concern and were assured that everything was fine. In her mind, she saw a car crash into a telephone pole. She noted the time, and her vision was at the exact time a wreck did occur. It was a cold, icy day, and O.V. had received an emergency call to go to the next town. A car skidding on the ice hit O.V.'s car, and he was forced into the telephone pole. He had a badly broken arm, and it took a while for him to recover, but he was more annoyed that it made more work for a lineman—he wished he had hit a tree instead.

O.V.'s success allowed his children to have a low key, gentle childhood, with schoolwork and friends, music lessons, and summer trips to see family in Jefferson and Vivian. The family also made occasional trips to the nearby Galveston beaches. There was always a negotiation over which car to take because Vina didn't like beach sand in her car.

Frederic and Rosemary were quite healthy, but Ruth was a sickly child and spent a lot of time as an invalid, with scarlet fever, malaria, and other ailments. One year she was given her Christmas and birthday presents in October because it seemed doubtful that she would survive until the end of the year. Her father spent hours playing games with her and shared his love of baseball, even taking her to local Houston Buff games when she was strong enough. She became interested in fashion while recovering and designed paper dolls for her amusement. Ruthie's parents continuously

O.V. & Vina, 1920's

prayed over this child and dug deeply into their faith. Their family doctor was daring (and desperate) enough to try an experimental injection treatment, and she miraculously recovered.

Reading was encouraged in their home, and there was a great deal of discussion over dinner about the books each person had read. A subscription to National Geographic had been purchased as soon as Vina knew she was pregnant, and as in many households, they saved them all. Because Houston offered many cultural opportunities, they whole family attended the symphony, ballet, opera and the theatre. Vina was most grateful that she was rearing her family there. The children enjoyed Saturday serial movies and playing with neighborhood friends. Ruthie excelled in school, as did Rosemary. Bubba never put forth the extra effort except in sports, especially pole vaulting. His mother's heart stopped when he was in the air, but they both managed to survive.

CHAPTER FIFTEEN

One More Move

Big changes were about to take place in the Summers family. In the fatal crash of the stock market on October 29, 1929, many investors lost all of their assets, resulting in many suicides. O.V. took some considerable losses, but nothing to cause him to take such drastic action. Even as the country settled into the Great Depression before World War II, Vina's allowance kept increasing, and O.V. purchased property in the well-established Southampton area near Rice Institute. He engaged an architect and builder, and the family soon moved into their substantial new brick home and new way of life.

Vina and O.V. both felt as though this house required upscale furnishings, so she set out to fill it with the best of everything. O.V. got more excited with every purchase and absolutely loved their new home. Of course, she loved it too, but the greatest attraction to her was the promise that this was truly the last move.

Vina had been happy where she was, but this new home was beyond anything she could have dreamed. O.V. wired the house himself. Unlike other homes being constructed in 1930, it had outlets on every wall, a large bathroom, elegant built-in cabinets, plastered walls and shiny woodwork, and their first electric refrigerator. As she wandered alone through the large rooms with high ceilings, the bedrooms with walk-in closets, the separate breakfast room and pantry, even the large room over the garage for Frederic, her emotions grew conflicted.

She sat down on a bench left by carpenters and reflected on how she had arrived at this moment in her life. On her first trip to Oklahoma, she had visited the dugout created by her father and brothers for shelter. It was where her family had lived in the dirt, where she was born, and where her mother died. Her father said that Melviney always loved having wildflowers in her home and they always made her smile. Vina also always kept fresh flowers in her home even though hers generally came from a florist. Vina had been told how her mother had prayed and hoped for a better life for her daughter, but she doubted her mother could even have imagined her only daughter's way of life. Vina's life, to others, appeared near perfect. What didn't show were the conditions and compromises that she knowingly, silently accepted day after day. She wondered, if taken in the contexts of their lives, was she really all that different from her mother?

Certainly, Vina had more creature comforts, but deep down in her soul where love grows, was her mother perhaps more fortunate? Melviney didn't have a husband return from business trips with a little less affection but bearing gifts; who had a wandering eye at every social event, and the gnawing doubts that Vina always had about his fidelity. With only that exception, he'd met the other conditions she requested before their wedding, allowing her to have her own money and a voice in decision making in most instances. He always provided her a car, and undoubtedly allowed more independence than most married women had at that time. In return, she always honored her commitment to him.

What Melviney did have was unconditional love from her husband. Their struggles appeared to have made the couple closer together; their lives were about survival which kept everything simple. As those times required, on the other hand, James was the undisputed head of his household, and his wife always bent to his ways. After making sure that everyone had food to eat and clothes to wear, the Knights were dedicated to educating their children as a way to improve their lives. Vina thought to herself, that is also what the mores of her day expected. It was always the easiest to just be subservient to the husband, and he will hopefully take care of his wife and family. Perhaps that would have been her path, Vina thought, had it not been for her abrupt ripping away from her family. A random thought came into Vina's mind: Feeling as though he was honoring her mother, having heard her many prayers, could it be that her father secretly arranged for her to be reared by someone else and tell no one? The notion troubled Vina. If that were so, she mused, why did Blanche try to hide her? It was not an impossible scenario, but she vowed to herself to never breach the subject to anyone. With that, she dismissed the idea. What did it matter now anyway?

Life's circumstances taught her when she was young to not count on anyone. Her mother's strength had come from her steadfast faith in God, and the words in her beloved Bible. Vina's relationship with God was ongoing and strong, and she was eternally grateful for HIS many gifts. She rose from the bench and set about the business of this one final move.

O.V. & Vina Summers,
New Neighborhood, 1930, Southampton

PART FOUR

Southampton, 2022

THE REST OF THE YEARS

After settling in, Vina and O.V. enjoyed getting to know their neighbors, most of whom were substantial members of Houston's elite. They joined the Second Presbyterian Church, and Vina became very active in children's charity work and her favorite group of women, Phi Omega Chapter of The Delphians, a group of about forty women studying the humanities at a college level. They met in the beautiful downtown Rice Hotel. The Delphians was tailored for women like her who had not attended college but sought further learning.

Eugenia, Arthur's mother, died in 1930, leaving just Arthur and Blanche to enjoy life in their final years together, especially touring around Northern Louisiana in his Maxwell. The Summers family made fewer visits to Vivian as the children got older and were involved in their various activities. Blanche died six years later after a short illness. Arthur was devastated. He was still a fairly young man but felt lost without his other half. Shortly thereafter, the white Victorian picturesque house on Forest Street burned to the ground. Absolutely nothing but ashes was left, with the exception of the mystery of how and why it was destroyed. Nothing was left of that house, but Vina's memories. Arthur was home at the time, and questions were raised: in his grief, did he accidentally or purposefully start the fire? No charges were filed, and no absolute cause was ever determined.

Vina played in several bridge groups and loved having parties, especially at home. She had a Negro maid, Louise, and always solicited Ruth and Rosemary to help her with the sometimes elaborate menus and decorations. O.V. planted a rose garden in the back of the house, and she rarely had to supplement bouquets with purchased flowers.

The move was easiest on Rosemary. She was full of confidence and quickly made friends so transitioning to a new school was easy for her, and she thrived. Ruthie's shyness was a challenge when she had to change high schools. She excelled academically, and her excellent piano skills helped her to enjoy parties once she broke the ice and made friends. She developed a small group of lifetime friends, and they played bridge together for over 50 years.

High school graduation came for Frederic after a laborious four years, and he vowed never to enter another classroom. O.V. arranged for him to work a couple of manual labor jobs to hopefully raise his aspirations. Neither job lasted very long, but when he found a job at a dental lab, he found his calling. His boss encouraged him to go to dental school, and he was quite the surprise student while flourishing in the mostly science classes. He graduated from the University of Texas Dental School the same day Ruth graduated from Rice with a degree in Romance Languages. Fortunately, one graduation was in the morning and the other in the afternoon. Frederic started a dental practice, while Ruthie had to go to Massey Business School to have marketable skills. O.V. still didn't think women should be in the workforce and would much have preferred she get married. She chose to continue to live at home, knowing her father would never have allowed her to move out.

Rosemary loved high school at San Jacinto and joined almost every activity available, becoming President of most. Frederic married Louise Redden from Shreveport, started a downtown dental practice, and built a home nearby. He went off to WWII as a medical officer and served in the Pacific Theater. He retired from the Navy as a Lieutenant Commander. He already had one son with another on the way when he was able to rent a suite of offices in a musty old bank building at the end of Main

Street to restart his dental practice. Shortly thereafter he had two serious heart attacks. After the second one, he gave up his Houston office, sold his home and moved to Ingram, Texas, where they already had a summer cottage. Settling into a slower pace of life, he started over with another practice, and their family immersed themselves in the community.

The WWII years found the country fighting on two fronts, and increasing demands were made on civilians. Worried about loved ones in the military, everyone avidly read the newspapers and magazines, and listened to the radio for war news. Rosemary had finished her industrious years at the University of Houston and was deeply in love with her army soldier, Owen McBride, from Oklahoma. Owen had already received his military orders, and she wanted to be with him while he was in the States. Just a few months after Pearl Harbor, they were married in a simple church ceremony with her sister as maid of honor. Ruth had fallen in love with a Dutchman, and as hard as he tried to join the U.S. military, he ended up with a job deferment, finding other ways to help the war effort. Another wedding took place a couple of months later. Same church, same dress, similar cake, just different bride and groom. Ruth and Fred Struben started their adventure together which soon took them to Ecuador, South America.

Vina became aware in her adult years that she did not have a birth certificate, having been born in Indian Territory. Since it was the norm for her husband to vouch for her, the lack of documentation was never an issue.....until it was! In 1949, perhaps it was only important to her, but she discovered a way to make it happen. Her brother Thomas, then 70 years old, had witnessed her birth, and she was able to get a notarized affidavit to that effect, presented it to authorities, and finally registered her birth.

All three of Vina and O.V.s children went on to lead productive lives. They produced four grandchildren, each of which had at least a bachelor's degree, one a master's degree, and one a doctorate.

After the war and all survived, life went on for everyone. O.V. and Vina had another twelve years together. They traveled extensively, and O.V.'s social activities, especially after retirement, were focused on the Texaco Country Club and golf. The news of their son Frederic's unexpected death of a massive heart attack at the young age of forty-five was shocking and devastating to the whole family. When children predecease parents, things are out of kilter, and Vina and O.V. both had trouble coping. Vina seemed to be grieving to the point of damaging her health.

As she continued to decline, her family finally convinced her to seek medical help, resulting in exploratory surgery which revealed widespread stomach cancer on August 22, 1957. The last eight months of her life were spent exactly as she chose. Feeling normal most of the time and overcoming it when she didn't with the help of medication, she reduced her activities and mostly focused on her friends and family. Reflecting on her life, she tried to imagine what was in store for the next generation and hoping that they would learn from the past. Her relationship with God was steadfast, and she had no fear of her fate. She read scriptures and her mother's Bible and had meaningful conversations with family and friends at her bedside. Vina distributed her belongings as she wished and participated in the Christmas holidays with her husband, children, and grandchildren. Her daughter, Ruth, lived nearby and visited almost everyday. Her last two weeks were spent in the hospital where she could be made more comfortable. O.V. buried his wife of forty-seven years in a beautiful spot alongside the luscious Sims Bayou, under a tree with a large granite stone. He stood there, when viewing the monument for the first time, grieving and contrite. Less than a year later, O.V. remarried. He visited there often and was buried by her side in 1963.

Vina , 1956

In Vina's own words, from a poem written shortly before she died.

Going Slowly

When one is leaving this life slowly, one ponders many things. What is it that causes the body to cling so tenaciously to life? Is it that life holds to the body with the fondness of a mother for a child?

Or does life love life and reluctantly let go of the many years of pleasure provided by the body, the dwelling place of life and spirit?

Why, when there is no further emotional need for life and all the spiritual needs have been fulfilled, does the separation of life and matter become such a struggle?

When the final chapter of life is written and the book is closed, what difference does the date make?

January, 1958 by Amanda Melvina Knight Summers

Author's note:

Vina remained a very independent woman of strong character throughout her life. That independence formed her life, and the lives of my mother, Ruth Louise Summers Struben, my aunt, Rosemary Vina Summers McBride, my cousin, Rosemary Vina McBride Sebastian, and my own, Amanda Felicita Struben Mims Hardick. She earned her independence the hard way. We learned from her example.

DEDICATION

I dedicate this labor of love to my granddaughters:
Samantha Ruth Mims who inherited Vina's abundant red hair
and indomitable spirit and to Elizabeth Angela Mims whose confidence,
compassion and multiple talents make the world a better place.
Your great-great grandmother, Vina, would be so proud of you both.

Samantha, 16 years old
Elizabeth, 7 years old
Vina, 19 years old

www.ingramcontent.com/pod-product-compliance
Lightning Source LLC
Chambersburg PA
CBHW041208150726
48006CB00016B/2164